Typesetting by:
N. Kessler

Edited by:
Naomi Music

As serialized in:

טלישראל

Distributed by:

Lechaim לחיים

Lechaim Productions Inc.
Tel: 718-369-2090, Fax: 718-369-2092
1529 Dean Street, Brooklyn NY 11213
info@lchaimusa.com
www.lchaimusa.com

©

All rights reserved.
Lechaim Productions Inc.
No part of this book may be reproduced
in any form, by any means, mechanical
or electronic, including photocopy,
translation and recording, without
written permission from the publisher.

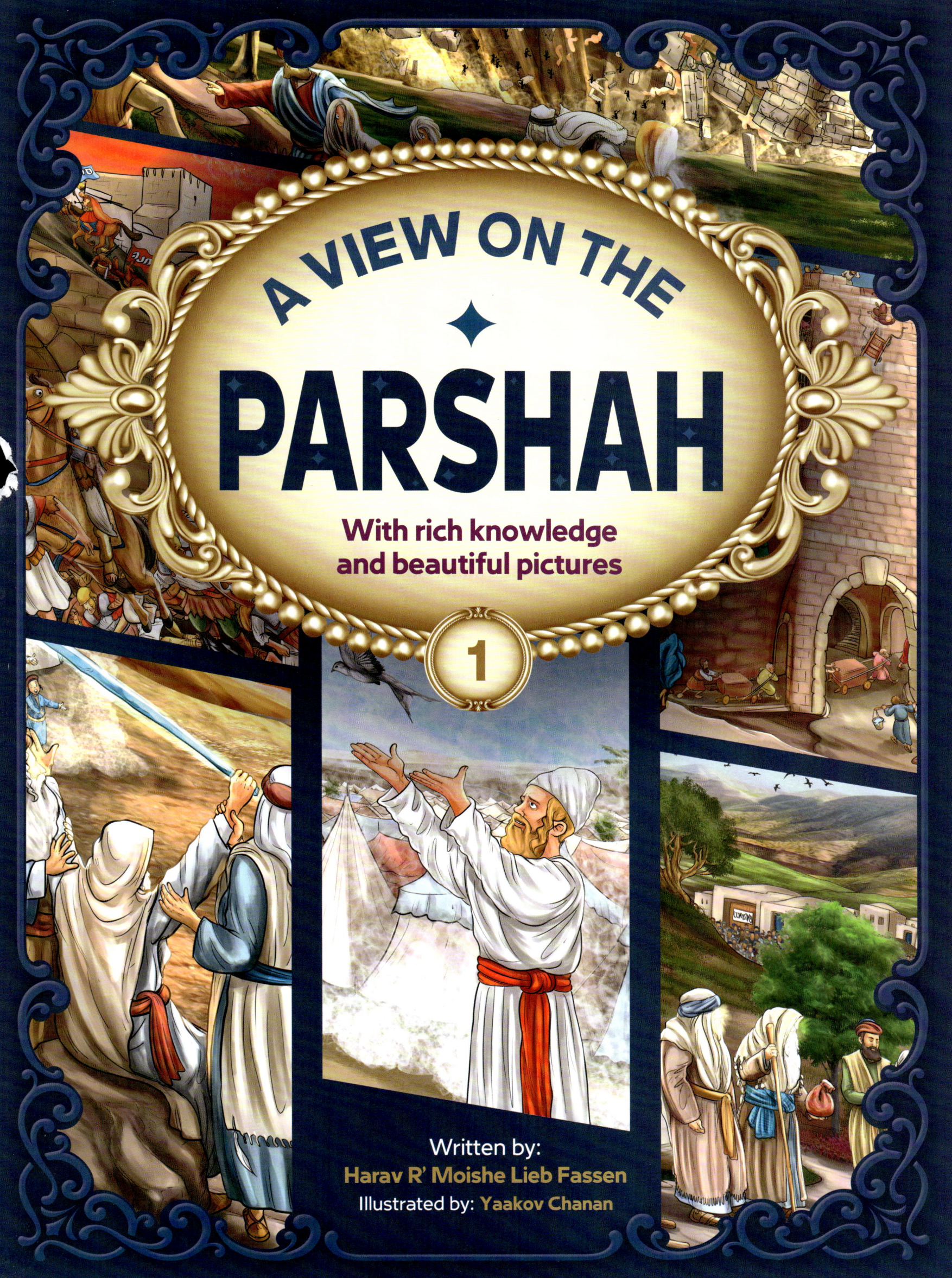

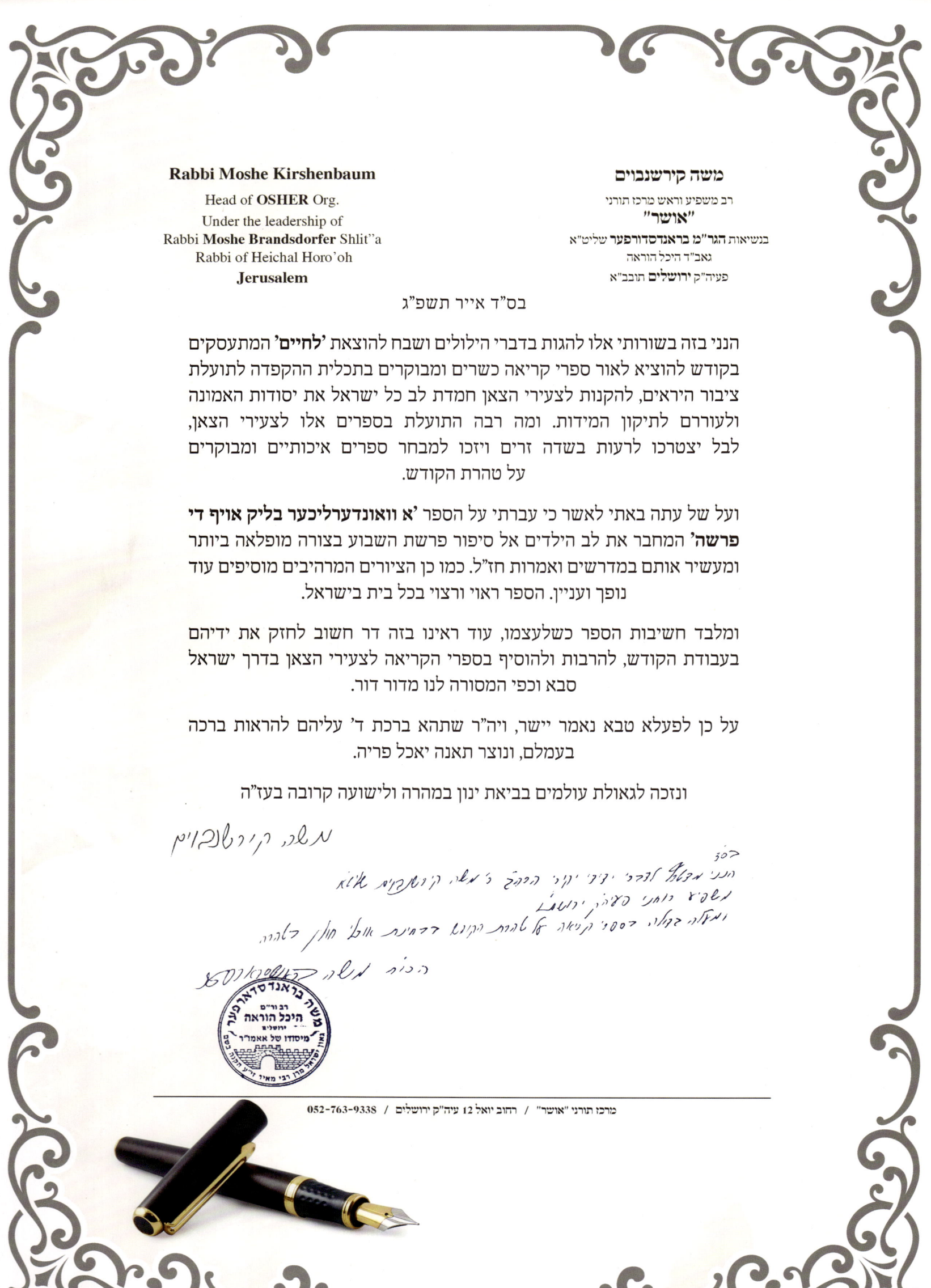

INTRODUCTION:

Dear Parents,

With gratitude to Hashem, we are excited to present this wonderful book, *A View on the Parshah*.

This is not just another book accompanied by masterful illustrations; this is a book you will enjoy giving to your children—a book that is full of Torah.

In this book, your children will read and learn new ideas and discover new Midrashim on the weekly *parshah*. They will familiarize themselves with these ideas and absorb the positive messages they contain. The beautiful illustrations will only enhance their interest.

We'd like to thank "Kindlein", a weekly publication, whose illustrations and ideas are enjoyed by so many readers.

Our goal at Lechaim is to publish beautiful and inspiring reading material for children. We are confident that this book will meet your expectations.

Enjoy reading!

LECHAIM

Question of the Week:
1. What in the picture was a miracle from heaven?

Kayin and Hevel

Adam began to settle in the world. He had five children: Kayin with his twin sister, and Hevel with his two twin sisters. Everyone did his role in the world. Kayin loved to sow and till the land; his brother, Hevel, loved to herd the sheep and cattle.

Hevel, who was cleverer than Kayin, engaged in more intelligent work. Although at that time man was not allowed to eat meat from animals, Hevel grazed the sheep in order to be able to benefit from their wool, milk, and cheese. Kayin and Hevel—being the only two brothers in the world—divided everything the world possessed between themselves. Kayin took for himself the earth to be able to sow and plant grain, while Hevel took for himself the living creatures, the cattle, and the animals to care for.

Kayin and Hevel got along quite well. Kayin gave Hevel some of his grain, and Hevel gave Kayin some of his animal fur and milk.

One day—14 Nissan—Adam called his sons to him and told them, "On this holy day our descendents, the Jewish people, will offer the *korban Pesach* to Hashem. It is worthwhile for you to also offer a *korban* to Hashem today."

Kayin and Hevel both went to take *bikkurim* from their possessions to offer as a *korban* to Hashem.

Kayin was very miserly, and instead of understanding that when you bring a gift to a king, you have to bring the most important things you have—the most beautiful and the best—he brought a little barley he had left over from his meal, together with a little flax, placed it on the *mizbeach* and waited for fire to come down from heaven, which would show that Hashem had accepted his *korban*.

Hevel understood that one should bring a *korban* of the most beautiful and best that one possesses. He brought the strongest and fattest animals, and sheep and cattle that had never had their wool sheared.

Suddenly, fire came down from heaven and burned Hevel's *korban*. The *korban* of Kayin, however, remained untouched. Hashem had not approved of it.

A strong anger burned inside Kayin like a fire. It was so strong that it caused him to want to take deadly revenge against Hevel. Instead of realizing that he had behaved wrongly and should learn a lesson from Hevel, he wanted to take revenge on his brother.

Besides his burning anger, Kayin felt very ashamed. He understood that it was not only the *korban* of Hevel that was accepted by Hashem, but also that Hevel was much more important to Hashem. This made Kayin feel rejected by Hashem.

Hashem appeared to Kayin, urging him to arouse and repent. "Kayin, why are you angry? Why are you ashamed? When a person makes a mistake, it is not good for him to think about his mistake and become broken. One should learn from it and work out how to correct it, so that next time will be better.

"If you improve yourself, you will *also* become more exalted, but if you throw away your chance, the *yetzer hara* is waiting at your door to make you sin again. Remember that if someone really wants to, he can fight his *yetzer hara* and prevail over it!"

But Kayin did not listen to Hashem's moral speech.

He only thought of how he could take revenge on his brother, Hevel. The opportunity was not slow in coming.

One day, while Kayin was in the middle of plowing a field, Hevel passed by with his sheep. Kayin fell into a rage. "What's going on here? Why are you coming to graze the sheep on my earth? The earth is mine!"

Hevel answered Kayin using similar language: "What's going on here? Why do you eat the cheese and drink the milk of my sheep? Why do you wear clothes made of sheep's wool? It is mine!"

"Get off my ground! Fly in the air!" Kayin yelled.

"Take off your clothes, which are made of my wool!" replied Hevel.

Thus began the war between the two brothers.

When people fight, there are always more things that come up to fight about. Kayin decided he couldn't let it go on like this. He had to take action. "I will kill him," Kayin thought to himself. "Then I will be the only child of my father, and the whole world will belong to me."

There was another benefit Kayin dreamed of. "The only reason Hashem did not accept my *korban* is because my brother, Hevel, is more important than me. If I kill him, and he is no longer here in the world, Hashem will be happy with *me*."

Hevel didn't realize how strong Kayin's anger against him was. He was not on his guard at all. So when Kayin asked him to go for a walk with him one day, he didn't suspect anything.

Kayin did not want to kill Hevel straightaway, as he didn't want his parents, Adam and Chava, to

Besides his burning anger, Kayin felt very ashamed. He understood that it was not only the *korban* of Hevel that was accepted by Hashem, but also that Hevel was much more important to Hashem. This meant that just as his *korban* was not accepted by Hashem, he himself was not accepted by the Him, because his *korban* was not accepted.

know what he was doing. He started talking to him about his feelings and how upset he was. He continued telling him how much he was hurt by the whole episode of the *korbanos*. He told him everything that Hashem had told him about repenting. And suddenly, without any warning, Kayin grabbed a rock and threw it at Hevel's forehead!

Hevel started to run away. Kayin ran after him. Over mountains and valleys, fields and forests, the two brothers ran, until they started fighting each other. But Hevel was stronger than Kayin. When he realized what Kayin wanted to do to him, he wanted to fulfill the words "להרגך השכם להרגו—*if someone comes to kill you, get up to kill him*." He threw himself on Kayin, and in just one moment Kayin was lying under him.

Kayin began to plead with Hevel. "I am begging you for mercy. Let me live. You are the only person in the world besides me and our parents. All will know that you are the one who killed me. What will you answer to our father?"

Hevel took pity on his brother and let him go. Kayin immediately jumped up onto Hevel… and killed him.

הבה נבנה לנו עיר ומגדל
Come, let us build for ourselves a city and a tower

A hundred and forty years had passed since the four families—Noach, Shem, Cham and Yafes, together with their wives—had walked out of the *teivah*. Since that time, children, grandchildren, even great-grandchildren had been born to them. A whole new generation filled the world.

The youth were not interested in following the ways of their great-grandfather, Noach—not even the way of their grandfather, Shem. All they wanted was to enjoy themselves in the manner of their own distorted understanding.

Nevertheless, in the back of their minds, they still realized that in the not-too-distant past there had been some advantages. All the people had felt like one family. They all spoke, the same holy language.[1]

Nimrod, the grandson of Cham, was a very great hero. He led wars, killed people, and conquered city after city, until he succeeded in becoming the one and only great king, who ruled over the whole world.[2]

One day Nimrod summoned all his great princes and sages to an urgent meeting.[3] "My noble lords," he began, "you all know that at this moment I am the greatest hero, the only king over all the people in the entire world. We must come up with a plan so that this will continue forever."

An important meeting was held at the king's palace, and each of the princes was asked for his opinion on how to strengthen Nimrod's kingdom. One of the princes said that in addition to the problem being dealt with, another problem needed to be addressed. Not long ago there had been a flood that had destroyed the world, and something needed to be done to prevent this from re-occurring.[4]

The prince's advice was to build a huge city with a mighty high tower.[5] "People like living in a place that has a special structure," he explained. "Many people will want to come and live in this special town. The tower will rise high above all the other buildings. Wherever someone goes in this huge city, he will be able to find his way with the help of the tower.[6] Even the shepherds outside the city, however far they need to go to pasture the sheep, will always be able to find their way back with the help of the tower.[7] And most importantly, it will serve as a good support for the sky. The tower will support the sky so that it will not split again and flood the world."

A second prince called out, "If we are going up to the sky, I think we should use the opportunity to attack it with big axes until all the water there runs out. Then there will be no need to worry about another flood."[8]

"My Lord, the King," they said to Nimrod, "everyone agrees to the plan to build a tower. There is only a difference of opinion as to what should be done with it. There are three opinions: 1) One group of princes says that when we get to the sky, an idol should be placed there so that he can take good care of us, looking down from so high above; 2) Another group says that once we get to the top, we should declare war with the Creator Who lives there (G-d forbid); 3) The remaining princes declared quite simply, "Why should we build a city on earth? Since we are going to heaven, let's settle there." King Nimrod approved the plan for the tower, and work began.

To build such a mighty, strong tower, a huge force of people was required. Six hundred thousand people came together to help with the work.[9]

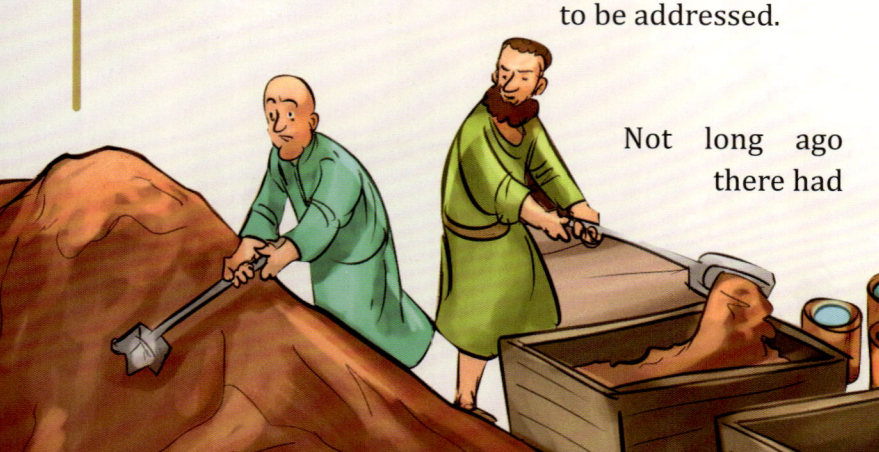

As there were no stones to build with, a huge factory was set up, with powerful, giant ovens, to make bricks.[10]

The tower had already reached seventy *mil* high. It took a year just to drag the bricks up to the top![11] From the east they went up with the building materials, and from the west they went back down to collect fresh building materials.[12]

King Nimrod himself, in all his glory and honor, came to visit. Even then, the workers continued to work, reluctant to waste even a second.

Hashem called together seventy angels from around His Kisei HaKavod, and ordered them, "Each one of you should take a family, enter their heads and make them forget the holy language, then plant a new language there." The angels did so, and it became a disastrous day—a plague of a mixture of languages.

"Pass a brick," someone shouted in Aramaic.

One day Nimrod summoned all his great princes and sages to an urgent meeting. "My noble lords," he began, "you all know that at this moment I am the greatest hero, the only king over all the people in the entire world. We must come up with a plan so that this will continue forever."

"Here is the axe," answered the second in Portuguese.

"I asked for a brick!" complained the first.

"Ah, do you need clay?" a third intervened in Russian.

"No, he needs rope," shouted someone from the bottom floor... in Persian.

And so the conversation continued, without anyone understanding what the other wanted.

Until, because of the confusion, people's heads, hands, and feet began to fly. Fighting started between them, and thousands of people fell like flies.[13]

Suddenly, one began to hear powerful thunder and lightning. The noise was strong enough to deafen people. Hail began to fall. The fear increased. People did not know where to run in order to escape. The huge, gigantic tower began to sink into the ground. All those who tried to run down and were in the lower third of the tower were buried alive under the ground.

1 Tanchuma Noach 19, Pirkei d'Rabbi Eliezer 24, Targum Yonasan v'Yerushalmi and Rashi in our *parshah*. 2 Pirkei d'Rabbi Eliezer 11. 3 Sforno 11:2. 4 Bereishis Rabbah 38:6. 5 Kli Yakar. 6 Or HaChaim Hakadosh. 7 Ibn Ezra 11:3. 8 Sanhedrin 109. 9 Sefer HaYashar. 10 Pirkei d'Rabbi Eliezer 24. 11 Sefer HaYashar. 12 Pirkei d'Rabbi Eliezer 24. 13 Bereishis Rabbah 38:10.

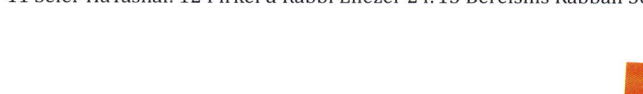

Answer for Parshas Bereishis:
Question: What in the picture was a miracle from heaven?
Answer: The fire that came down from heaven to consume the *korban* from Hevel.

LECH LECHA פרשת לך לך

Questions of the Week:
1. Most of the sheep look different. How many can you find that look exactly the same?
2. Look carefully at the picture. Which are the shepherds of Avram, and which shepherds belong to Lot?

ולא יכלו לשבת יחדיו

They were not able to dwell together

After Pharoah kidnapped Sarai, and Hashem severely punished him, he sent them all away with a large fortune.

"Listen, Avram, take your wife and get out of Mitzrayim. It is a very corrupt place, and I cannot take any responsibility for what will happen to you. Sarai can keep all the gifts I have given her. You too can keep everything you have received from me. I will give you still more gold and silver, more sheep and cattle, so that you will forgive me and you will have food to eat in Canaan."

The return journey took much longer than the journey there because they had to travel with extra sheep and cattle. Finally, after three months, Avram arrived back at his tent, between Beis Kel and Ai. The *yeshivah* was set up again, and Avram continued to spread *emunas Hashem*.

Dozens of shepherds were needed to tend Avram's sheep, and dozens were needed to tend Lot's. One day a shepherd came to Avram completely bruised and wounded. Avram, being the kind and compassionate person that he was, could not bear to see a wounded man. He got up quickly and ran towards him. "Perhaps I can help you with something to ease the suffering?" he asked worriedly. "Tell me quickly, how did this happen? Is one of the neighbors upset with us? Who hit you like that?"

"My master, Avram," the shepherd began, "I want to explain to you what has been happening day after day. You know that we have a difficult job providing grass for so many sheep and cattle to graze. We start work very early. We go out with the sheep to look for a place that is empty and *hefker*—ownerless—and let the animals graze in those fields. As soon as we are settled, along come Lot's shepherds with all their animals, and they enter the field we worked so hard to find."[1]

"My dear shepherd," Avram answered, "you have learned from my home for so long. Do you not remember discussing the matter of being a מעביר על מידותיו—*a person who works on themselves*? Even if they are doing something wrong, you still do not have the right to fight, especially as we are new to this area. When the neighbors see us fighting among ourselves, they will think of us as wild people and drive us out of here!"[2]

"Sir," replied the shepherd, "we didn't fight, and I didn't get hurt because of that. We *did* go to graze in another field. That's how it was for a few days. We didn't say anything to Lot's shepherds, so as not to start any dispute. But today we couldn't contain ourselves any longer. We saw how Lot's shepherds let their sheep graze in the fields of the Canaanim. Real robbery!"

"Robbery?" Avram was shocked. "Tell me quickly what transpired. I can't allow something like this to happen here, especially since Lot looks like me. People will say that the Avram who tells everyone to behave honestly is not honest himself,[3] and they will stop listening to my lessons in faith. Tell me quickly what you saw."

"My dear master," the shepherd answered, "we stopped the shepherds of Lot because they were grazing in the field of a Canaanite. Hear what they answered. They said that Hashem has given Eretz Yisrael to Avram, and since Avram has no children, and Lot is his heir, they may use all of the land!"

"Oh, woe!" Avram began to cry bitterly. He

immediately called Lot. "Listen to me," he begged him. "Things can't continue like this! Firstly, your shepherds are fighting with mine over the fields and where to graze. If the neighbors hear how many sheep we have, they will come and kill us in order to seize our property.[4] Secondly, if the neighbors hear the lie your shepherds are saying—that Eretz Yisrael is ours—that alone will be enough reason for them to come and kill us.[5] In fact, your argument is not at all justified; Hashem *did* promise to give Eretz Yisrael to my children in the following generations, but until now I have not been privileged to have children, and the land is not yet mine."

"So what do you want, Uncle? What should I do?"

"Listen, Lot, we can no longer live together. Choose a place to live, and we will remain good friends from afar."

"Look, Uncle," said Lot, "you are so righteous, you are scared of the slightest sign of theft. Here, among the area of the cities, there is a small town, Sedom, a really nice place. In it live people who are not so

"Listen, Avram, take your wife and get out of Mitzrayim. It is a very corrupt place, and I cannot take any responsibility for what will happen to you. Sarai can keep all the gifts I have given her. You too can keep everything you have received from me. I will give you still more gold and silver, more sheep and cattle, so that you will forgive me and you will have food to eat in Canaan."

particular about stealing...[6] I hear it is very good there... I think it is the right place for me to settle."

"Lot," Avram replied, "go where you want... I'll go the other way."

"Yes, that's what I really wanted to speak with you about, Uncle. Don't even come near me... Not only in Sedom, but promise me you will not even come to the adjoining cities."[7]

"I agree, Lot, and I will tell you one more thing: Since you started stealing, the Shechinah has not appeared to me.[8] Perhaps if you leave this place, I will once again merit having Hashem appear to me. Nevertheless, I beg you, Lot, remember all the good things I taught you."

Annoyed, Lot moved away from Avram's home. "I don't need Avram or his G-d," he angrily announced. He moved to Sedom. He didn't actually live in the city of Sedom, because coming from the holy home of Avram, he was unable to live in such immorality. He settled outside the city, near the gate.[9]

1 Ramban 13:7, Sforno 13:7. 2 Sforno 13:7. 3 Yalkut Me'am Loez. 4 Ramban 13:7. 5 Kli Yakar 13:7. 6 Kli Yakar 13:7. 7 Ramban 13:12. 8 Kli Yakar 13:14. 9 Chizkuni 13:12.

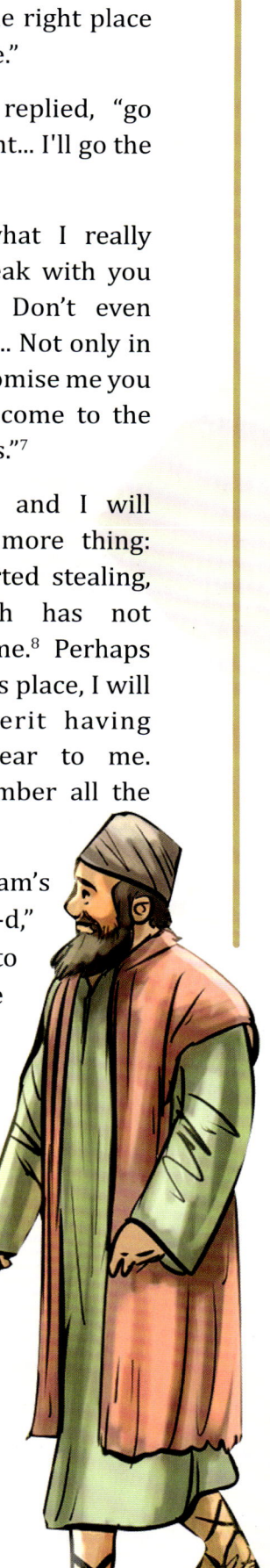

> ! **Answer for Parshas Noach**
> Question: Did the whole tower sink?
> Answer: The upper third burned, the lower one sank, and only the middle one remained.

VAYEIRA פרשת וירא

Question of the Week:
1. What time of day was Sedom overturned?

הפיכת סדום
The overthrowing of Sedom

Lot was the chief judge, and he sat at the main entrance of the city. Regardless of how bad he was, he still had goodness inside him from when he had lived in Avraham Avinu's house. So when he noticed the *malachim*, it was only natural that he wanted to take them into his house as guests.

Although he wanted to take them in as guests, he knew the kind of town he was in; and as a judge, he also knew the laws that dealt with people who committed the terrible offense of taking in a guest. He called the *malachim* quietly to one side and began to plead with them, "I beg you to come and spend the night in my house."

Everything would have passed peacefully, if not for Iris, Lot's wife. Even though Lot had secretly brought guests home at night many times before with no problem, tonight Iris did not agree. When Lot asked her to prepare a meal for the guests, she refused to do so. Without any choice, Lot went into the kitchen, rolled up his sleeves, and prepared a meal for the *malachim* himself. They washed for the meal, and Lot put down fresh *matzos* that he had baked *l'kavod Pesach*. Then he brought in the other delicacies he had prepared.

Iris was not at the feast. She was busy with a cruel plan. She went from neighbor to neighbor. "Can I borrow some salt? We have guests, and I want to prepare a good meal." It didn't take too long for her trick to work... and the whole town—from big to small, men, women, children, and old people—gathered in front of Lot's house. "Give us the guests!" they shouted. "You have hardly lived here, and you became our judge... and in the end you don't even obey our laws! Here with the guests!"

Lot tried to plead with them, but the people became wilder by the minute. "You *golem*! You fool! Move to the side and let us get to the door! We know what to do with your uninvited guests!"

When the *malachim* saw that things were getting out of control, they pulled Lot into the house, and at that moment, the assembled crowd went blind. They did not know what had happened. They searched blindly for the door, in order to get into Lot's house, but to no avail. They became tired and gave up.

The *malachim* said to Lot, "Listen, until now we weren't certain that Hashem would really ask us to overthrow Sedom. We still thought there was a possibility He would find some merit towards the people. But after this, we clearly see what kind of city exists here, so quickly take your wife and children and sons-in-law, and together we will escape before it's too late."

Lot tried to persuade his sons-in-law to join him, but they made fun of their old father-in-law who believed what the strangers had said about the city being destroyed overnight.

"Hashem has heard Avraham's *tefillah*," the *malachim* told Lot. "The city of Zo'ar will be saved, but now we need to get you out of here immediately, before it is too late."

Lot fell into a fear. He literally became paralyzed. He could not walk. The *malachim* grabbed him and dragged him out of Sedom, and they started running.

> *Lot's wife heard the sounds of Sedom being destroyed and could not bear the thought of all her money being burned there. She also still hoped to see that her two other daughters were following them. She looked back... and there was nothing more left of her than a mound of salt.*

"No one should look back!" the *malachim* warned. "Whoever looks back could be included in the destruction!" The *malachim* grabbed hold of Lot, his wife, and his two daughters and rushed them away.

Malach Gavriel grabbed the stone on which Sedom and the other cities lay and gave it a shake. Fire and brimstone began to rain from the sky. Gavriel turned the stone over, and in an instant, Sedom became a piece of history. Nothing more than a little dust remained.

Lot's wife heard the sounds of Sedom being destroyed and could not bear the thought of all her money being burned there. She also still hoped to see that her two other daughters were following them. She looked back... and there was nothing more left of her than a mound of salt.

Answers for Parshas Lech Lecha
Question: 1. Most of the sheep look different. How many can you find that look exactly the same?
Answer: Five.
Question: 2. Look carefully at the picture. Which are the shepherds of Avram, and which shepherds belong to Lot?
Answer: The shepherd lying on the floor wounded is wearing blue and brown clothes. All the shepherds wearing the same clothes must belong to Avram, and the others to Lot.

מערת המכפלה
The Cave of Machpeilah

When the three *malachim* came to visit Avraham Avinu on the third day of his *milah*, it is written in the *passuk* that Avraham prepared three oxen in order to give each one of the guests a tongue, the finest meat from the animal.

In the *passuk* it says, "ואל הבקר רץ אברהם—*Avraham ran to the cattle.*" Simply put, the *passuk* means that Avraham hastened to fulfill, as quickly as possible, the *mitzvah* of *hachnasas orchim*.

The Zohar HaKadosh says that one of the oxen ran away from Avraham Avinu, and he followed it until Chevron, where he caught up with it at a cave. This was Me'aras HaMachpeilah. Avraham saw two people lying on a bed. Candles were burning, and it looked like they were sleeping sweetly. It was Adam and Chava.

Avraham then smelt the smell of Gan Eden and saw an extraneous light shining in the cave. Hashem then revealed to him that the special light in the cave was due to the fact that Adam and Chava were lying there. Avraham felt a strong desire to bury Sarah Imeinu and himself there after their deaths.

This story is also mentioned in *Perkei d'Rabbi Eliezer*, and in *Baal HaTurim Al HaTorah*. It is noted that "ואל הבקר" has the same letters as "ואל הקבר," which alludes to the story written in the Zohar.

A great sadness reigned in the country because of the death of Sarah Imeinu, since as long as she lived, everyone in the country was successful in everything they did. So when she passed away, everyone cried and mourned her death. Avraham Avinu comforted them. "Don't grieve, my children," he said. "This is how the world works. Everyone, whether righteous or wicked, eventually leaves the world."

On the day Sarah Imeinu died, all the people closed their businesses. Everyone stopped working, and the whole city came to pay their last respects to the righteous Sarah, who was appreciated and respected by all.

Everyone gathered at Ephron's field and watched as Avraham tried to negotiate the purchase of the place he desired as a burial place for his wife.

The Bnei Cheis paid great respect to Avraham Avinu and said, "You are a president of G-d among us! Choose the best place from us here

> The Zohar HaKadosh brings down that one of the oxen ran away from Avraham Avinu, and he followed it until Chevron, where he caught up with it at a cave. This was Me'aras HaMachpeilah. Avraham saw two people lying on a bed. Candles were burning, and it looked like they were sleeping sweetly. It was Adam and Chava.

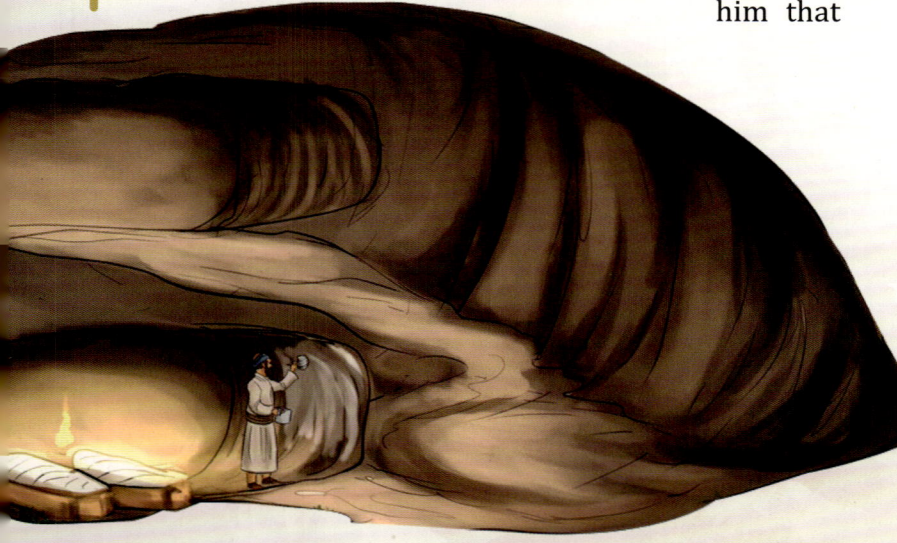

in the city in order to bury Sarah." In the merit that they honored Avraham in this way, there was no war in their country as long as he lived.

Avraham bowed and thanked the Bnei Cheis and asked them to talk to Ephron—the owner of the field in which Me'aras HaMachpheila was situated—and persuade him to agree to sell the field with the cave.

Hashem arranged that on that very day Ephron was chosen to be the mayor of the city, as it would be an honor for Avraham to deal with a mayor rather than just a simple person.

Ephron was a big swindler. He acted friendly towards Avraham. "I am offering you, my master, my whole field without any payment. Completely free!"

"G-d forbid! I should take something from a person for nothing?" Avraham answered. "Just tell me the price, and I'll pay you the full value!"

"My master," Ephron answered, "what is a piece

On the day Sara Imeinu died, all the people closed their businesses. Everyone stopped working, and the whole city came to pay their last respects to the righteous Sarah, who was appreciated and respected by all.

of land worth only 400 shekels between such good friends as you and me?"

Avraham understood the hint... and counted out the entire amount for Ephron, despite the fact that it was a large amount of money. Not only did he do that, he also paid him in a currency that was worth a lot and was accepted everywhere in the world.

All those gathered were witnesses to the sale, and a deed was written stating that from now on Avraham was the owner of the field with the cave. Avraham ordered that the cave be plastered over and prepared to bury Sarah Imeinu inside.

Sarah's funeral was celebrated with great honor. Her bed was carried by the most important people of that time, among them Shem ben Noach, his son, Ever, Avimelech the king of the P'lishtim, Enor, Eshkol and Mamrei, and many other personalities of the country.

Answer for Parshas Vayeira:
Question: What time of day was Sedom overthrown?
Answer: At sunrise.

פרשת תולדות TOLDOS

Question of the Week:
1. Find the hidden letters in the picture and put together words that

ויתרוצצו הבנים
And the children fought together

We learn in this week's *parshah* that Rivkah was worried because her children, Yaakov and Eisav, were fighting each other. Rashi learns from Chazal that they fought over the two inheritances: Olam Hazeh and Olam Haba. In the end they divided them: Yaakov took Olam Haba for himself, and Eisav took Olam Hazeh.

Rabbi Mendel of Riminov told the following story:

"One day Eisav was riding on his beautiful horse and carriage, enjoying Olam Hazeh in the fullest sense of the word, when suddenly a terrible frost descended and a stormy wind began to blow. A blizzard blew outside, and a heavy snow fell, which froze the whole area.

"Eisav was frozen to the depths, and his bones were trembling with cold. He could not bear the terrible weather. To add to all his troubles, his horse slipped off the road and sank into the mud, so he could barely move.

"As he didn't have a lot of food with him, he needed to be careful with what remained, so he ate and drank just enough to sustain himself.

> "Eisav was frozen to the depths, and his bones were trembling with cold. He could not bear the terrible weather. To add to all his troubles, the horse slipped off the road and sank into the mud, so he could barely move.

"This continued for several days, he struggled greatly to find shelter for himself.

"Suddenly, he saw a light shining in the distance. Oh, how much he rejoiced. 'I will be able to warm my bones a little and come back to myself.'

"Coming closer, he noticed that the building was a *beis medrash*, and on it was written 'Yeshivas Beis Yaakov Avinu.' He looked inside and saw that his brother, Yaakov, was leading the *yeshivah* and teaching his students. They were in the middle of learning Bava Kamma and were dealing with a difficult subject with many Tosfos. As the students were busy studying together with their rabbi, Yaakov, a fire was burning in the shul and a pleasant warmth radiated.

"As soon as Eisav saw this, he fainted on the spot. Immediately, the students ran and helped him; they carried him to the stove and gave him a warm plate of soup, until he was revived and his heart was refreshed.

"When he had completely recovered, he began to argue with Yaakov. 'You fraud! We made an agreement that I get Olam Hazeh and you only have Olam Haba. I won't get Olam Haba, but I definitely don't have Olam Hazeh either. All day long I wander around with my horse and carriage in the woods and fields, I have to go to all the dangerous places to catch animals, I'm dying of hunger and cold, and you—who are not supposed to have Olam Hazeh—are sitting in a beautiful, warm building, surrounded by hundreds of students. Winter is nice

and warm here. Summer is pleasant and airy. There is no shortage of food and drink. Where is the justice? You are breaking our agreement!'

"'Listen, Eisav,' answered Yaakov. 'Your arguments are 100 percent right, and I'm ready to trade with you. You give me your horse and cart, and I'll give over the entire *yeshivah*, with all the students, right now.'

"Eisav smiled to himself, 'Yaakov is so naive. He is once again doing foolish business.' Yaakov took the horse and cart, and he left the *yeshivah* to Eisav.

"The day was over, the next day had arrived, and all the students were sitting in the *beis medrash* waiting for their rabbi to come and give them their *shiur* and continue explaining the difficult Tosfos from the day before.

"After a while, a few students entered the new *rosh yeshivah*'s room and asked him, 'When is the rabbi coming to class? The crowd is already waiting.'

"'You know that I have barely regained my *kochos*—strength—from my difficult journey. It doesn't seem that I will be able to give a shiur today.' So

"Coming closer, he noticed that the building was a *beis medrash*, and on it was written 'Yeshivas Beis Yaakov Avinu.' He looked inside and saw that his brother, Yaakov, was leading the *yeshivah* and teaching his students. They were in the middle of learning Bava Kamma and were dealing with a difficult subject with many Tosfos. As the students were busy studying together with their rabbi, Yaakov, a fire was burning in the shul and a pleasant warmth radiated everywhere.

Eisav excused himself from teaching.

"Some time passed, and the students began leaving the *yeshivah* to seek out Yaakov. When Eisav was left alone in the *beis medrash* and there was no one to heat the *yeshivah*, he became cold again. Hungry and thirsty, he thought, 'It was better when I could ride my horse. At least I could hunt for something to eat. I think I should switch back with Yaakov.'

"However, Yaakov did not agree so quickly. 'It is your decision to give up being the *rosh yeshivah*, but I will not give the horse and cart back. Business is business.'

"Eisav had no choice, and he left with an angry face and empty hands."

Answer to Parshas Chayei Sarah:
Question: Where else do we find a cave with a bed in, and a light that burned at the time of someone's death?
Answer: At the death of Aharon HaKohen.

Questions of the Week:
1. Which *malach* did not have the right to enter the city of Luz?
2. What wonderful thing happened in the city of Luz?

וישכם במקום ההוא
And he lay down in that place

The story taught in this *parshah* is certainly known to everyone. Therefore, we will concentrate mainly on the innovations in the picture, and on the Midrashim from which they are brought down.

The story in brief: Yaakov Avinu went to Charan. Arriving there, he realized that he had passed Har HaMoriah, the place where his parents had *davened*, and he had not *davened*. So he turned back and retraced his steps with the intention of reaching Yerushalayim. But when he arrived at the city of Luz, Hashem performed a miracle, and Har HaMoriah jumped towards him.

Hashem made night fall two hours early, and Yaakov Avinu lay down to sleep on the earth and dreamed the famous dream with the ladder.

Before going to sleep, Yaakov took twelve stones from those that his grandfather, Avraham Avinu, had used to build the *mizbeach* in order to sacrifice his father, Yitzchak, and he placed them around his head to protect himself from wild animals.

had used to build the *mizbeach* in order to sacrifice his father, Yitzchak,[1] and he placed them around his head to protect himself from wild animals.[2]

He placed one stone under his head, one stone on each side of his head, one more behind his head, and a fifth above his head.[3] He placed the remaining seven stones around his body.

The five stones around his head began to quarrel among themselves. Each stone claimed, "The *tzaddik* should lay his head on me!" Hashem performed a miracle, and all the five stones joined together and became one big stone. The remaining seven stones had not fought, and therefore they remained separate.[4]

In his dream Yaakov saw a huge ladder standing on the ground near the city of Beersheva, and its top reached to the heaven above the city of Luz. Because Har HaMoriah had come to him, he saw in the heaven, right at the top of the ladder, the heavenly Beis HaMikdash, which is located directly opposite the Beis HaMikdash down here on earth.

He saw *malachim* going up and down the

ladder. These were the two *malachim* who had come in the form of men to destroy Sedom. Since they had greeted Lot and said, "We [which could be understood as 'not Hashem'] are going to overturn Sedom," they were punished: their wings were cut off, and they could not return to heaven.[5] Now they tried to go up to heaven on the ladder in the dream, but they were sent back down. These were the *malachim* that Yaakov later sent to Eisav in Parshas Vayishlach.[6]

The five stones around his head began to quarrel among themselves. Each stone claimed, "The *tzaddik* should lay his head on me!" Hashem performed a miracle, and all the five stones joined together and became one big stone. The remaining stones had not fought, and therefore they remained separate.

Yaakov Avinu had a staff with him that was hollow and contained oil. He was able to light a candle with it so that he could learn at night. This was the staff that Eliphaz had left him with when he had escaped to Charan.

It also states in the Midrash that while Yaakov Avinu was in Charan, and grazing Lavan's sheep, he recited verses of Tehillim.

The city of Luz was very interestingly built. It was surrounded by walls on all four sides, and it was not possible to enter it. In front of the city stood a huge tree, which had an opening in it through which one entered a cave under the ground, and only through that tree and the cave could one enter the city.[7]

In the dream, Hashem showed Yaakov the four periods of galus—*galus Bavel, galus Madai, galus Yavan* and *galus Edom*—and promised that his children would be redeemed from all four of them. Now we are in the last *galus*—*galus Edom*—and we hope to be redeemed very, very soon, through HaMelech HaMashiach!

1 Pirkei d'Rabbi Eliezer. 2 Rashi. 3 Rashi on Midrash. 4 Divrei David. 5 Midrash Rabbah. 6 Shach on the Torah. 7 Yalkut Me'am Lo'ez.

Answer for Parashas Toldos:
Question: Find the hidden letters in the picture and put together words that are related to the story.
Answer: עולם הבא, עולם הזה

VAYISHLACH פרשת וישלח

Questions of the Week:
1. How many kings can you find in the picture?
2. Do you know the names of the kings, and the cities in which they reigned?

מלחמת בני יעקב
War of the sons of Yaakov

In this week's *parshah* we learn about the capture of Dinah by Shechem, and how Shimon and Levi, being only 13 years old, waged war with the entire city of Shechem and killed all its inhabitants.

The Midrash writes that when Shimon and Levi slaughtered the entire city of Shechem, fear fell on all the people around Shechem, and they said, "If just two of Yaakov's sons can do this, what might be accomplished if all of Yaakov's children would get together. They would be able to destroy the whole world!" A fear of the G-d of the Bnei Yaakov came upon them, and they did not dare go out to fight with them.

However, the Midrash adds a continuation to the story. Despite the fact that the townspeople did not oppose the Bnei Yaakov at that time, seven years later, when the Bnei Yaakov went to graze their sheep in the city of Shechem, the kings said, "Isn't it enough for the sons of Yaakov that they killed all the inhabitants of Shechem? They still want to inherit it too?"

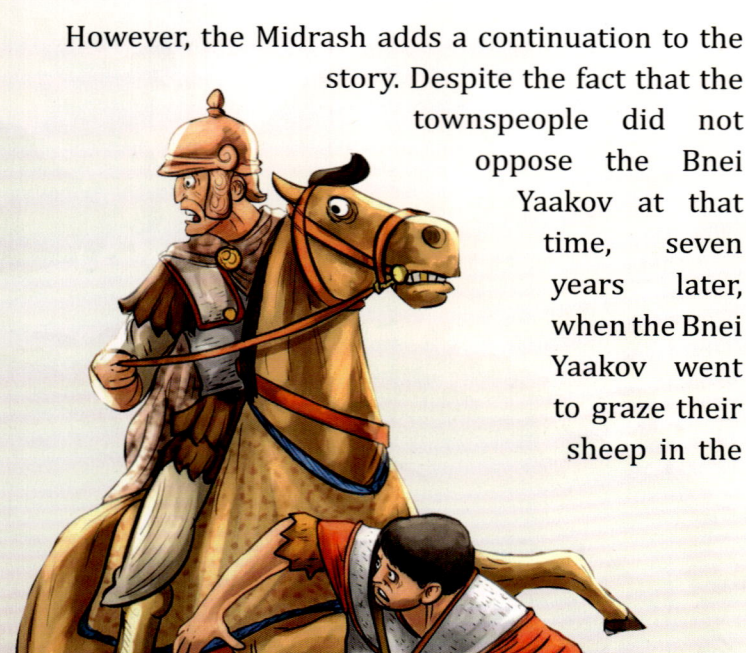

All the kings of the area decided to gather together and fight against Yaakov and his sons.

As soon as Yehuda saw them, he jumped into the midst of the enemy's army with his sword and began killing them until he saw himself standing opposite King Tapuach.

King Tapuach was completely covered, from head to toe, in an iron and copper armor. He was a very brave and strong king. He rode on his beautiful horse, and at the same threw spears with his two hands! With one hand he threw spears in front, and with his other he threw spears behind—and he always hit his target. He was such a great hero that he scared everyone.

Even though Yehuda saw this famous mighty hero, armored from head to toe and throwing spears in both directions, he was not afraid. While running towards him, Yehuda picked up a huge stone—the weight of sixty *sela'im*—and, jumping high, he threw it at the king's head. The giant hero fell from his horse.

Tapuach still tried to put up a fight, but Yehuda, with his bravery and strength, defeated him and killed him.

Seeing what had occurred, the nine friends of King Tapuach came to attack Yehuda. Yehuda kicked a stone and knocked the head of one of them. He then grabbed his shield and killed the other eight.

Then Levi killed Alon, the king of Geash, and Yaakov Avinu killed Zahori, the king of Shiloh. The rest of the kings became very frightened, lost their motivation to continue fighting, and ran away. The sons of Yaakov chased them until night, and Yehuda killed thousands of them.

The rest of Yaakov's sons came out of the ruins of Shechem and followed the army until the city of Chatzer, where the war became more intense. The four remaining kings were killed by Yaakov's arrows.

The war that Yaakov's family waged with the mighty kings and their people continued for several days. The rest of the people, they took into captivity, together with their possessions. They collected all the possessions and goods belonging to the enemy, packed them in sacks, and took them for themselves.

On the sixth day of the war, the survivors gathered together and came to Yaakov Avinu without any weapons. They bowed at his feet and asked for peace. Yaakov Avinu willingly agreed to make a peace agreement with them on condition that they would undertake to pay taxes for Yaakov and his children.

King Tapuach was completely covered in an iron and copper armor, literally from head to toe. He was a very brave and strong king. He rode on his beautiful horse and at the same threw spears with his two hands! With one hand he threw spears in front, and with his other he threw spears behind—and he always hit his target. He was such a great hero that he scared everyone.

When they came back from the war, Yaakov asked, "Who do you think did the most in the war?"

"Father," they answered, "you are much older than us. What were you able to do?"

Yaakov Avinu said to them, "Now I will show you who has more power." He took them to the gate of the city, locked it well, and said to them, "Push!"

They all started pushing the gate with all their strength, but they were unable to open it. They admitted that it was only due to their father's merit that a *nes* had happened and they had won the war.

Answers for Parashas Vayeitzei:
Question 1: Which *malach* did not have the right to enter the city of Luz?
Answer: The Angel of Death has no control over, nor the right to enter, the city of Luz.
Question 2: What wonderful thing happened in the city of Luz?
Answer: Whoever found himself in the city of Luz never died.

VAYAISHEV פרשת וישב

Question of the Week:
1. Why did the Shevatim dye Yosef's shirt specifically with goat's blood?

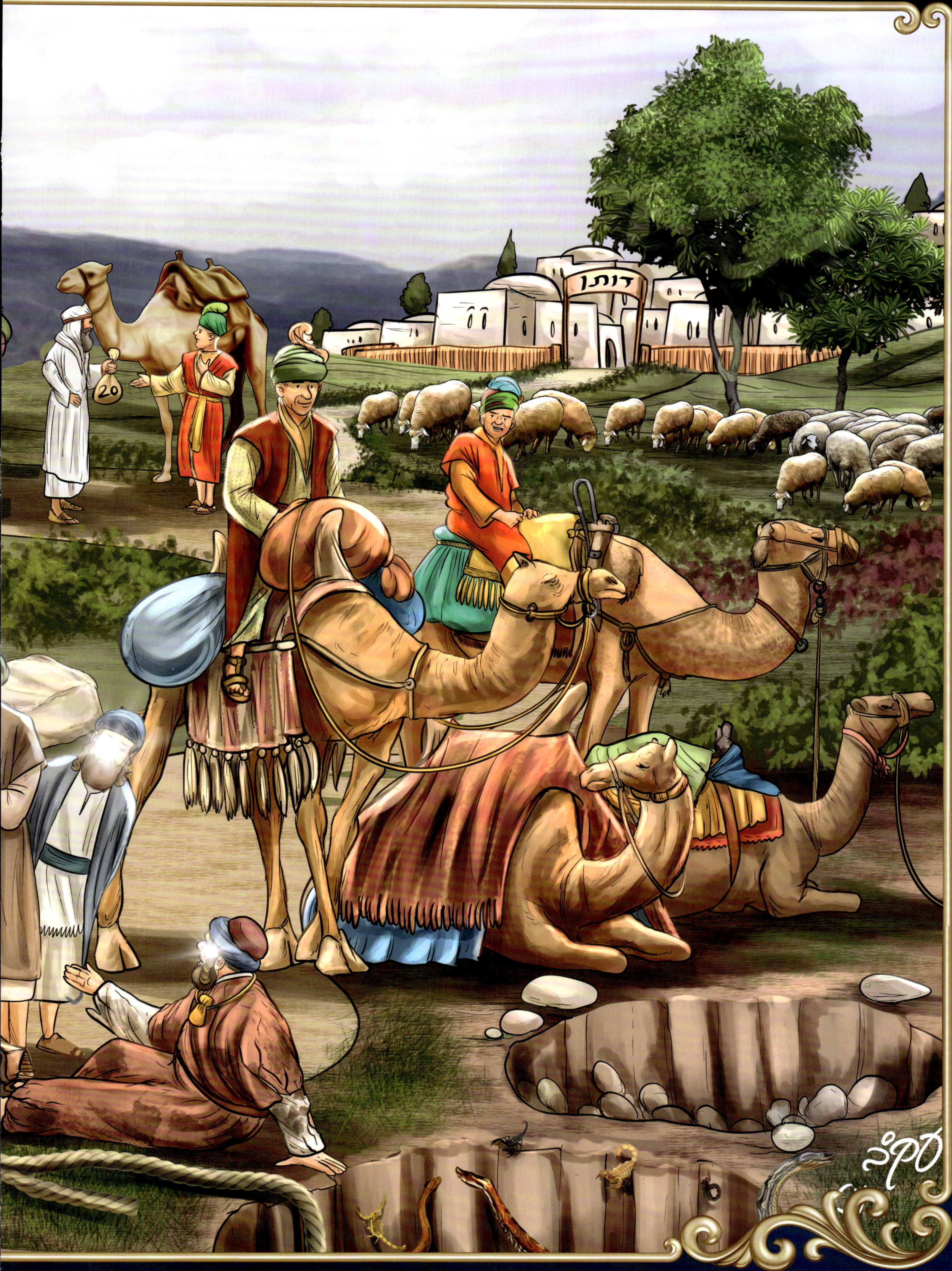
דותן
20

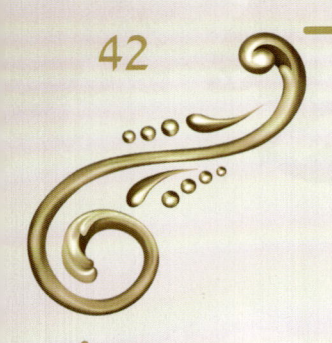

מכירת יוסף
Sale of Yosef

Introduction:

Dear children, before we start writing about the sale of Yosef, we must preface the following:

Studying the Torah is not the easiest thing to do; you have to struggle to understand it. But the most difficult and most sensitive *parshiyos* are apparently the ones that deal with Yosef's dispute with his brothers.

We have no understanding of the *kedushah* of the Shevatim of Hashem, the Shevatim from whom the whole of Klal Yisrael descends, and even though we learn about the sale of Yosef as a common brotherly quarrel, we must know with certainty that this story is not at all as superficial as it appears to us, with our limited understanding! It is much, much higher and holier—too deep for us to comprehend.

However, the Torah has given us permission to learn it simply as we see it written, but we must remember that this is not the true story.

Let's describe it as we see it in the picture.

Shimon and Levi claimed that according to *halachah* Yosef deserved to be sentenced to death. When Yosef arrived in Dosan, they believed that it was the right time to accomplish this. Reuven, in an attempt to save Yosef, said that they should throw him into a pit.

Shimon and Levi claimed that according to *halachah* Yosef deserved to be sentenced to death. When Yosef arrived in Dosan, they believed it was the right time to accomplish this. Reuven, in an attempt to save Yosef, said that they should throw him into a pit.

There were two pits there. One pit was full of stones, and the other was full of deadly snakes and scorpions.[1]

There are two ways in which the Mefarshim explain the story:

One opinion is that Reuven wanted to save Yosef, and that's why he wanted to throw him into the pit with the stones, planning to come back later and save him. But the brothers threw Yosef into the second pit, with the snakes. It was there that Hashem made a miracle, and the snakes and scorpions did not even touch Yosef.[2]

The second opinion is that Reuven argued with the brothers that even though they really believed Yosef deserved to die—because he was a rebel against the Kingdom of Yehuda, and according to the *halachah*, such a rebel deserves death—perhaps a mistake had been made in their judgment and he would be killed falsely. They said that the snakes and scorpions, which have no free will, would not be able to hurt Yosef if he was not destined to die. They said, "Let us throw him into their pit, and we will see what happens to him. If they kill him, it will be a sign that he is truly committed to death, and if not, it is a sign that he is not supposed to die." Hashem made sure that neither the snakes nor the scorpions touched Yosef.[3]

The brothers had another complaint against Yosef. He was slandering them to their father, regarding eating *eiver min hachai* (a limb from a living animal). The truth was, however, that the Shevatim could have created an animal using holy names, and regarding such an animal the prohibition does not apply. It therefore appeared to Yosef that they were eating without slaughtering.

After throwing Yosef into the pit, the Shevatim sat down to eat a meal. Yehuda could not eat because of great grief. He cried bitterly and could not console himself.[4] He complained to the brothers that they had behaved mercilessly toward Yosef.

Meanwhile, a group of merchants passed by, and they dragged Yosef out of the pit. The brothers wanted to sell Yosef to them, but since Yosef's clothes were badly torn and he looked very sickly after lying terrified in the pit, the merchants did not want to pay for him. In the end they agreed to buy Yosef for a pair of shoes.

Yosef had an amulet around his neck, and Malach Gavriel pulled out brand new clothes from it. Yosef looked like a new man. A group of Arabs passed by, and when they saw Yosef, they understood his worth and bought him from the merchants for twenty shekels.[5] Meanwhile, the brothers slaughtered a goat and dipped Yosef's shirt in its blood, and they sent it to Yaakov Avinu, saying, "This is what we came across..." And from this Yaakov understood that a wild animal had attacked him.

Reuven was not present at the sale of Yosef, as he was busy doing *teshuvah* for the mistake he had committed regarding Bilha.

> The brothers had another complaint against Yosef. He was slandering them to their father, regarding eating *eiver min hachai* (a limb from a living animal). The truth was, however, that the Shevatim could have created an animal using holy names, and regarding such an animal the prohibition does not apply. It therefore appeared to Yosef that they were eating without slaughtering.

1 Midrash Rabbah. 2 Divrei Yo'el. 3 Zohar HaKadosh. 4 Midrash. 5 Midrash—Da'as Zekeinim.

Answers for Parshas Vayishlach:
Question 1: How many kings can you find in the picture?
Answer: Seven.
Question 2: Do you know the names of the kings, and the cities in which they reigned?
Answer: Tapuach; Alon, king of Gesh; Zahori, king of Shiloh; Praton, king of Chozer; Susi, king of Sarton; Lavan, king of Katron; Shachir, king of Machana.

MIKEITZ פרשת מקץ

Question of the Week:
1. Find four words hidden in the picture that are related to the picture.

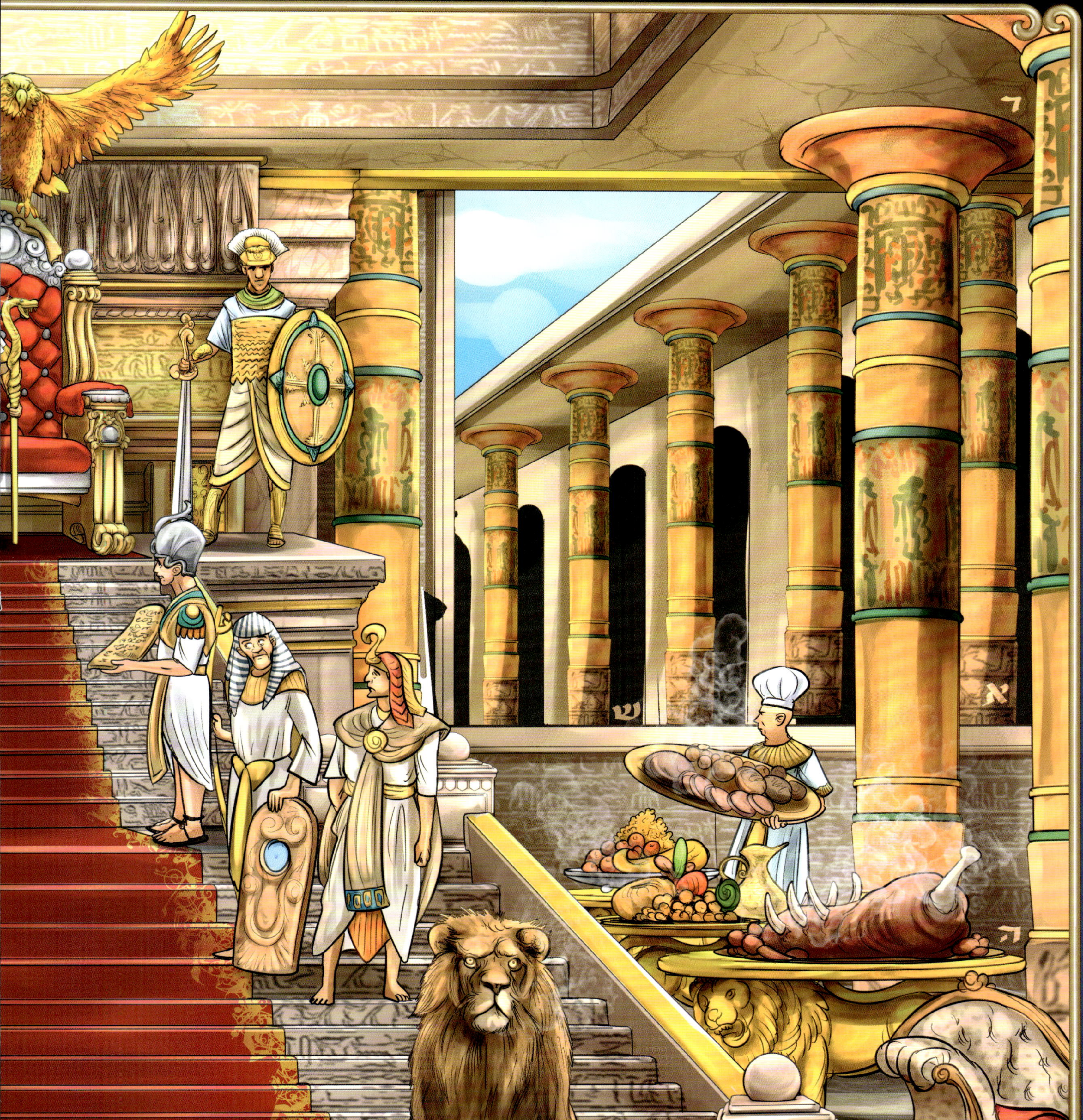

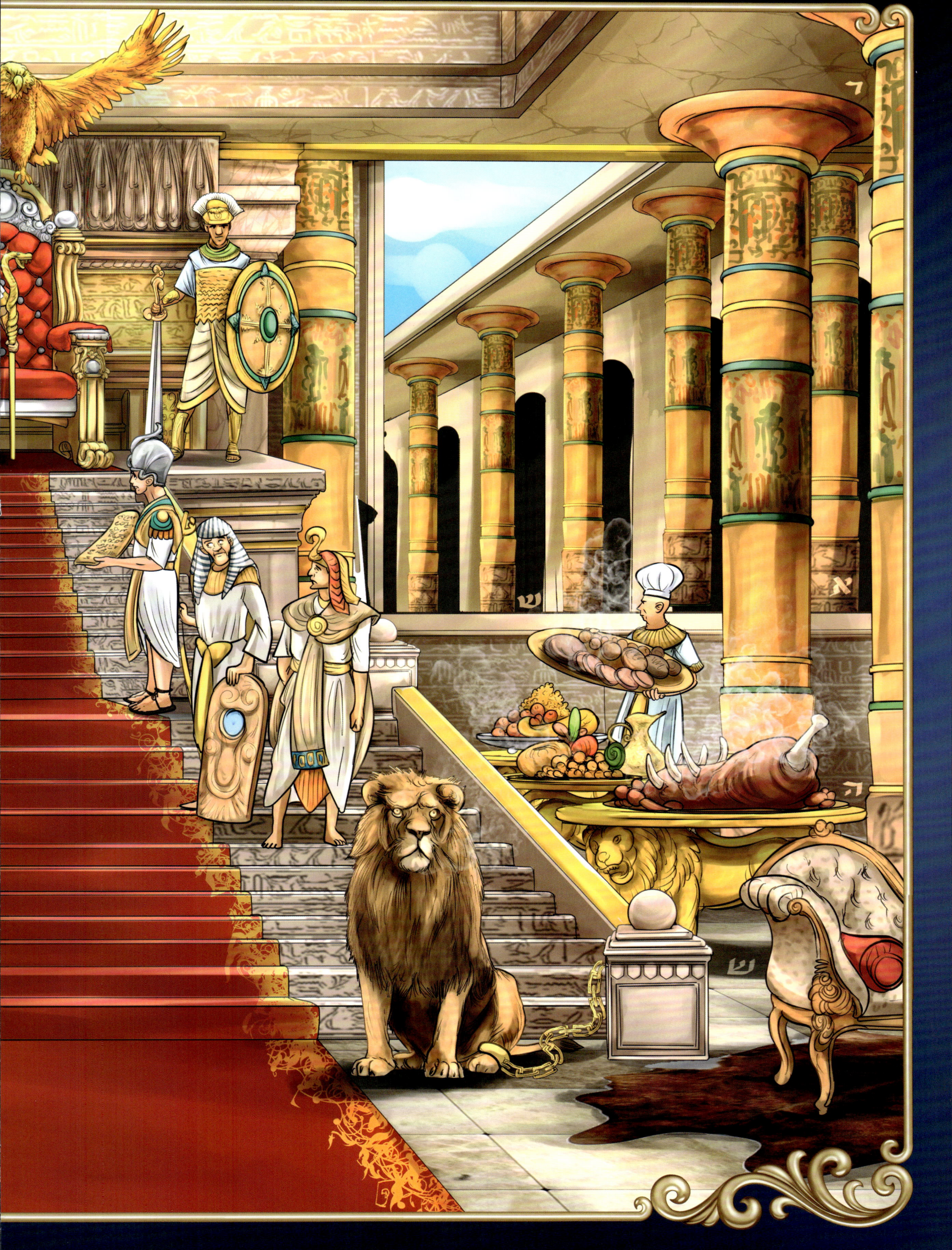

מקץ שנתיים ימים – יום הולדת פרעה
The end of two full years — Pharaoh's birthday

Last week we learned at the end of the *parshah* that Yosef interpreted the dreams of the chief butler and the chief baker.

The *passuk* tells us that Pharaoh used to prepare a great feast in honor of his birthday. The Midrash says that Pharaoh used to sit at the feast dressed very royally. He wore very special, glamorous clothes, with an eye-catching crown on his head. This crown was set with extraordinary precious stones that gave off a most beautiful shine. Everyone who looked at Pharaoh wearing his royal outfit was full of wonder.

Pharaoh sat on his high throne, which had seventy steps. When someone wanted to talk to Pharaoh, he was not allowed to ascend to the top of the throne. The greater the visitor was, the higher he could climb the steps, and the closer he could get to Pharaoh.

Exactly two years after the chief baker and the chief butler were taken out of prison it was once again Pharaoh's birthday. The story with Pharaoh's dreams happened then, so it turned out that Yosef was actually released from prison on the day of Pharaoh's birthday. In *Sefer HaYashar* it is written that Hashem planned it just like that because Pharoah received new servants and government employees only once a year, on the day of his birthday, and Yosef had to become the Mishne LaMelech—second in command to the king.

Exactly two years after the chief baker and the chief butler were released from prison it was once again Pharaoh's birthday. The story with Pharaoh's dreams happened then, so it turned out that Yosef was actually released from prison on the day of Pharaoh's birthday. In *Sefer HaYashar* it is written that Hashem planned it just like that because Pharoah received new servants and government employees only once a year, on the day of his birthday, and Yosef had to become the Mishne LaMelech—second in command to the king.

It was not only Pharaoh's birthday, but the whole world celebrated its birthday... It was Rosh Hashanah, the day the world was created, and as we say on Rosh Hashanah when *davening*, "היום הרת עולם—Today is the birth of the world."

But one minute... A birthday?

Isn't this a *goyshe* thing?

Isn't this talking about the wicked Pharaoh?

What does this mean for us, Jewish children, the chosen nation?

A good question!

And the Gemara says that when the *goyim* celebrate their birthday, it is a matter of idolatry. In *Meshech Chochma*

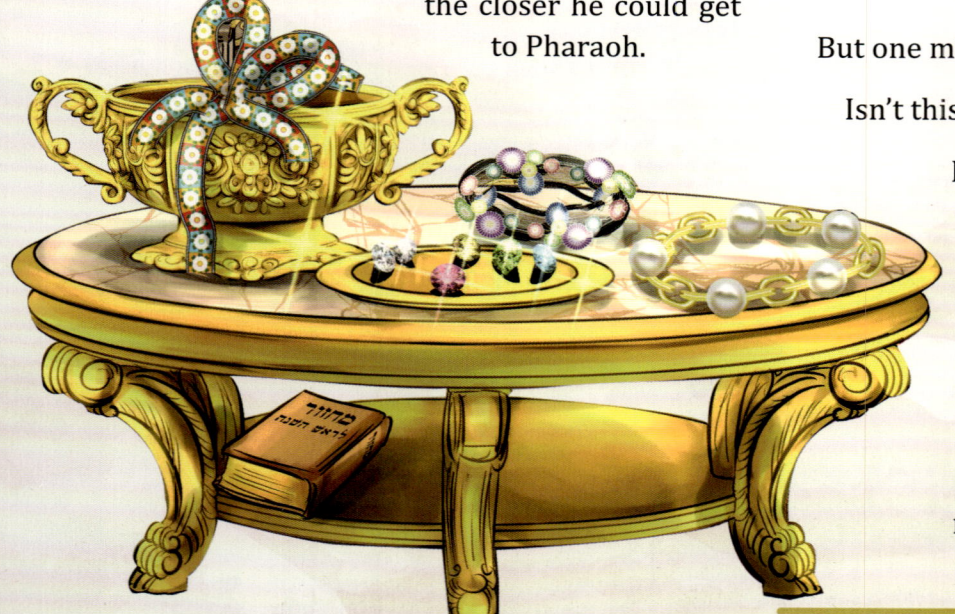

an interesting thing is written: Yosef did not greet Pharaoh, unlike what we find by Yaakov Avinu. As it was Pharaoh's birthday, Yosef did not want to give him honor while he was busy with idolatry!

It is indeed generally accepted that celebrating a birthday is only found with Pharaoh, a *goy*, and it does not apply to us, Yidden.

But let's look a little deeper into the matter. Is this really the only time we find the subject of birthdays in Tanach and Chazal? Do you perhaps remember that in the merit of a birthday we have the happiest day of the year, the great Yom Tov Purim? Yes, children! Haman wanted to kill the Yidden on 7 Adar, which is when Moshe Rabbeinu died. What did he forget, children? Yes, yes! You remember well! He forgot that on this day, Moshe was also born, and this brought about the miracle of Purim! The Gemara[1] even expresses that 7 Adar is a day of feasting and joy, because of Moshe's birthday!

We also find in Chazal special importance in the months when the Avos were born, and at other times when certain *tzaddikim* were born, such as David HaMelech.

> And the Gemara says that when the *goyim* celebrate their birthday, it is a matter of idolatry. In *Meshech Chochma* an interesting thing is written: Yosef did not greet Pharaoh, unlike what we find by Yaakov Avinu. As it was Pharaoh's birthday, Yosef did not want to give him honor while he was busy with idolatry!

So we see from Chazal that the day of birth is a great day.

The *Sefarim HaKedoshim*, therefore, also explain that the day of birth is indeed a great day! But it depends on how you celebrate it. The *goyim* don't have any boundaries. They behave inappropriately and make whole feasts. So the day is a wasted day. In contrast, if one behaves like an *ehrliche* Yid, by thanking Hashem for all the good He does for us and *davening* to Hashem with special concentration and enthusiasm, then the day has a special importance.

---

1 Nazir 14.

Answer for Parshas Vayeishev:
Question: Why did the Shevatim dye Yosef's shirt specifically with goat's blood?
Answer: Because its color is the most similar to human blood.

VAYIGASH פרשת ויגש

Question of the Week:
1. What did Yosef want to hint to Yaakov by sending the wagons?

חיים רהט

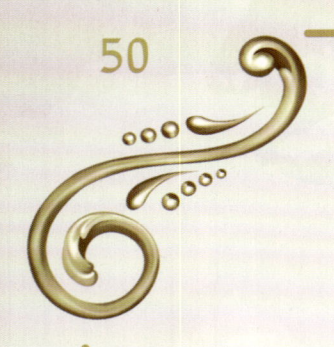

וירא את העגלות
And he saw the wagons

"Yosef's brothers have arrived!" stormed one of the servants in Pharaoh's palace. "And not just brothers… They are very important people from the land of Canaan, grandchildren of the world-famous Avraham."[1]

Pharaoh quickly sent over all the ministers and servants to celebrate with Yosef. The whole army, along with all the officers and important people, came to the palace of Yosef HaTzaddik, where it was happy and lively with the discovered brothers of the Mishne LaMelech.[2]

Pharaoh sent word to Yosef, "Tell your brothers to bring everything they own to Mitzrayim, and they should settle here! They should go back to Canaan, pack all their possessions and goods, put their families and their father on the wagons I will send you, and as soon as possible move to Mitzrayim. I will give them the best place in the country to live in."[3]

Pharaoh actually sent over eleven wagons. When Yehuda saw the wagons, he started shouting, "Avodah zara! The wagons have pictures of idols! We will not use the tamei wagons!" Yehuda made a fire and burned the wagons. Yosef quickly came back with fresh, clean, kosher wagons.

Pharaoh actually sent over eleven wagons. When Yehuda saw the wagons, he started shouting, "*Avodah zara*! The wagons have pictures of idols! We will not use the *tamei* wagons!" Yehuda made a fire and burned the wagons.[4] Yosef quickly came back with fresh, clean, kosher wagons.[5] In addition to all the carriages, Yosef added the magnificent royal carriage in which he had ridden throughout Eretz Mitzrayim on the day he had become the Mishne LaMelech. Now it was to be used in order to bring his father, Yaakov.

Yosef gave each of the brothers new clothes.[6] He gave them not just simple clothes, but glorious royal clothes.[7]

Yosef also provided each of his brothers with ten servants who would serve them on the way to Canaan, help them pack up, and bring their families down, with their belongings, to Mitzrayim.[8]

Binyamin received 300 coins from Yosef, after which he divided magnificent royal clothes decorated with gold and silver. Yosef ordered everyone to put on their royal clothes, and with their royal clothes on display, they went to greet Pharaoh. Pharaoh received them with great joy, especially when he saw that the brothers of the assistant to the king were all heroes and appeared so royal.[9]

Yosef also made sure that beautiful clothes were packed for his brothers' children. Each one of them received a beautiful royal dress and 100 coins. The women in the palace were also ordered to send clothes decorated with gold and silver and precious diamond stones for his brothers' wives. To his father, Yaakov, Yosef sent the royal clothes that he himself had worn on the day he had become the king's assistant in Mitzrayim.[10]

Then Yosef packed them provisions for their journey. He took ten donkeys, one for each of the brothers to take care of, besides Binyamin, whom he didn't want to give any extra work to.[11] He loaded the donkeys with all the good things Mitzrayim possessed, then he took ten more donkeys and loaded them with grain, bread, side dishes to eat with the bread, delicious, aged wine that old people love, beans, figs, raisins, beans, and lentils, and other tasty food.[12]

Arriving home in Eretz Yisrael, Yaakov's children decided it would be dangerous to tell their elderly father that Yosef, whom he had been missing and grieving for for around twenty-two years, was living a very healthy and pleasant life and was the king in Mitzrayim. They would have to plan how to reveal everything slowly, so that Yaakov would be able to digest the good news easily.[13]

Serach, the daughter of Asher, was just passing by.

"Serach, we have marvelous news from Mitzrayim. Uncle Yosef is alive, and he himself is the king of Mitzrayim! Serach, you can sing beautifully and play the fiddle. Please go in to your grandfather, Yaakov, with your fiddle and sing a beautiful, calm song for him. You should include the words 'Yosef lives' and 'Yosef is the king in Mitzrayim,' so that he will catch the good news!"

1 Radak. 2 Sefer HaYashar. 3 Sforno. 4 Midrash Rabbah. 5 Yalkut Me'am Lo'ez. 6 Alshich HaKadosh. 7 Sefer HaYashar. 8 Yalkut Me'am Lo'ez. 9 Sefer HaYashar. 10 Yalkut Me'am Lo'ez. 11 Rashbam. 12 Sefer HaYashar. 13 Rishonim.

Answer for Parshas Mikeitz:
Question: Find four words hidden in the picture that are related to the picture.
Answer: ראש השנה יום הולדת

פרשת ויחי VAYECHI

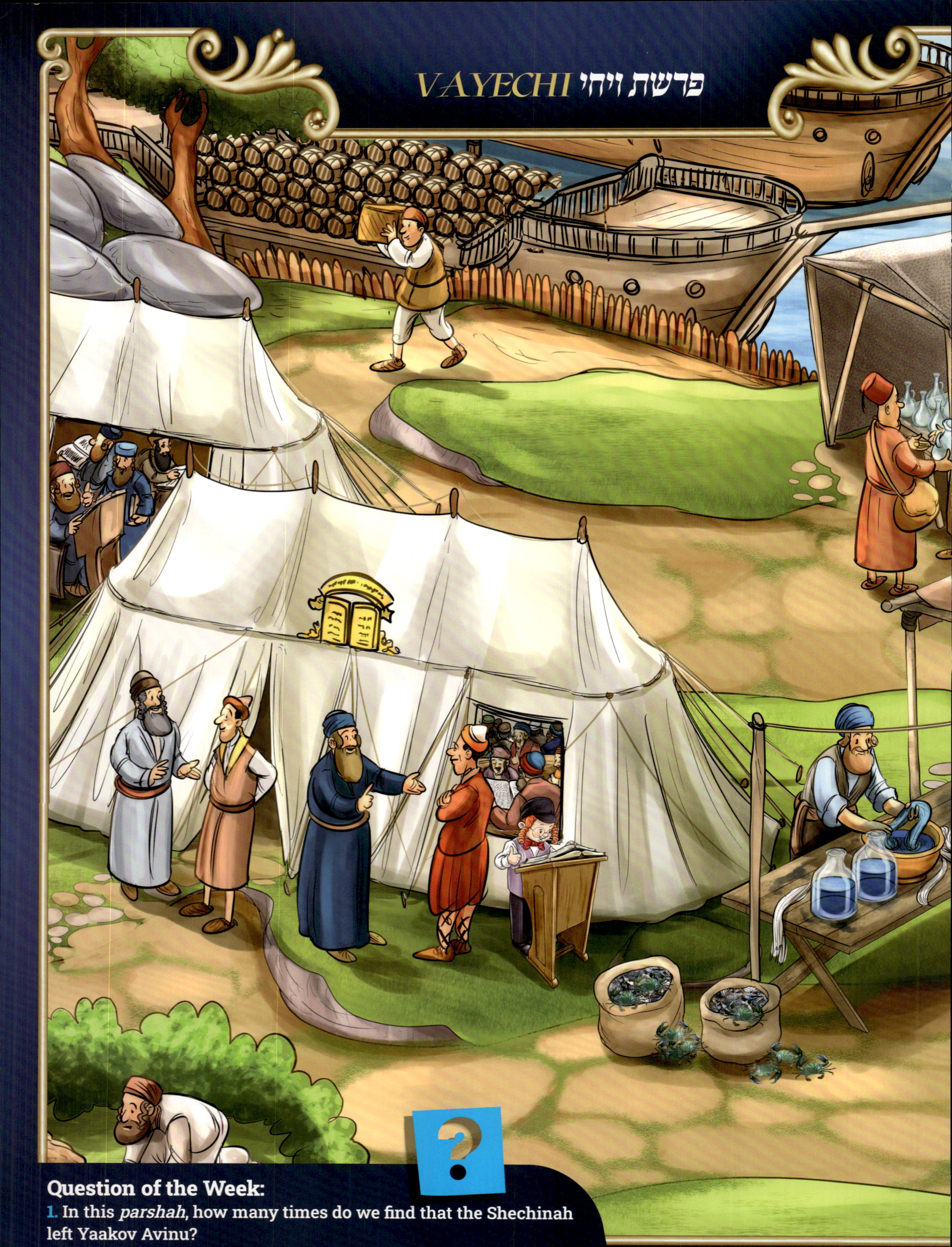

Question of the Week:
1. In this *parshah*, how many times do we find that the Shechinah left Yaakov Avinu?

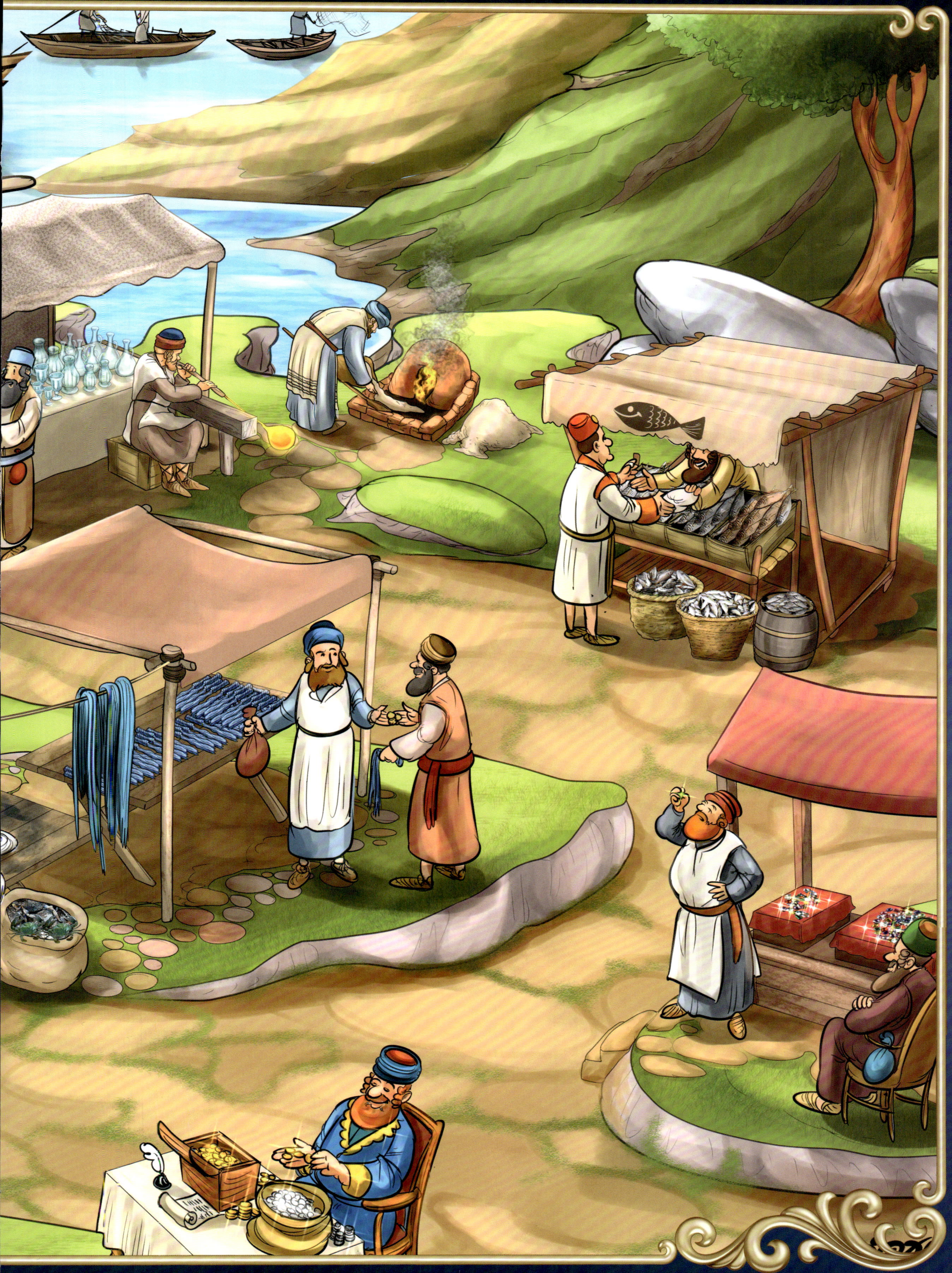

זבולון לחוף ימים ישכון
Zevulun shall live at the seashore

Even though Yissachar was older, Yaakov blessed Zevulun first because Shevet Zevulun supported Shevet Yissachar, enabling them to sit and learn. (Moshe Rabbeinu also did the same.) From this we learn that one who supports *talmidei chachamim* receives *brachos* both in this world and the next world:[1] wealth this world, and reward for the Torah in the next world.

The *brachah* given to Zevulun was that the land he would receive in Eretz Yisrael would be by the sea. He should not worry that his share would be less than that of the other Shevatim because, on the contrary, at the sea he would earn very handsomely. Firstly, the port is where all the ships bring their goods, and he would be the one managing the entire trade at the port,[2] and secondly, he would have his own ships and would be able to import his own goods through the port.[3]

Both Yaakov Avinu and Moshe Rabbeinu blessed Yissachar and Zevulun simultaneously for another reason. Through both of them together, Klal Yisrael were able to be *mekadesh* the month—it was Shevet Zevulun, who were usually at the seashore, who were repeatedly witnesses for the Sanhedrin when checking for a clear moon, and the Sanhedrin themselves, the ones sanctifying the month, originated from Shevet Yissacher.[4]

Zevulun would also find various precious treasures in the sea, from which they would become very rich. For example, there was the *chilazon* fish—needed in order to dye the *tzitzis* blue—which everyone would buy from them.[5] The *chilazon* was very expensive because it appears on the sea's surface only once in seventy years.[6]

Zevulun would also find a very special sand that could produce precious glass. Shevet Zevulun would be the only owner of that glass, and anyone who wanted it would have to buy it from them. This would also bring them in a nice income.[7] They would also find treasures of pearls in the sea,[8] and whales would spit out onto the seashores of Zevulun all the treasures they had swallowed from sunken ships: precious vessels, gold, silver, and diamonds.[9]

They would be so rich that they would dig pits in the sand in order to be able to hide their great wealth.[10]

Hashem promised Zevulun that despite the fact that the sea is in the open, no one would be able to steal from them, because whoever would take away from his possessions without paying would

Rabbi Itzik'l Pshevorsk zt"l used to distribute kugel on Shabbos morning after davening. Naturally, the floor became dirty from it. Once, after dividing the kugel, the Rabbi called out, "Chassidishe yingelech... and you aren't catching any kugel!" The Yidden looked around in amazement, not seeing a scrap of kugel left on the table. Pointing his fingers to the floor, the Rabbi called out, "There are treasures on the ground! Why don't you pick them up?" The Rabbi didn't give up until all the trodden kugel was picked up from the floor!

not succeed and would lose everything.[11]

"Yissachar," Yaakov Avinu said, "will bend his back in order to take on the burden of the Torah, and will strive to understand its deep secrets."[12]

The *goyim* who came to trade with Zevulun would say, "As we are already in Eretz Yisrael, let's go up to Yerushalayim and see the Beis HaMikdash."

They would see the extraordinary beauty and splendor of the Beis HaMikdash and all the Yidden serving the one and only G-d, and all eating the same food. They would become so impressed that they would want to convert.[13]

What was this one food?

It is remarkable what Rabbi Eizik'l of Kamarna *zt"l* writes: that the food was *kugel*, which is eaten and enjoyed by Yidden on Shabbos Kodesh.[14]

Rabbi Meir'l of Premishlan *zt"l* said that eating noodle *kugel* on Shabbos Kodesh is "הלכה למשה מסיני—halachah *given to Moshe at Sinai [for which there is no reference in the Torah].*"[15]

Zevulun would also find various precious treasures in the sea, from which they would become very rich. For example, there was the chilazon *fish—needed in order to dye the* tzitzis *blue—which everyone would buy from them. The* chilazon *was very expensive because it appears on the sea's surface only once in seventy years.*

Reb Mendele of Riminov *zt"l* said the *kugel* eaten on Shabbos will be placed on the scales and counted among our merits in the next world![16]

The Choize of Lublin *zt"l* said that in the next world there is a special room where those who eat *kugel* on Shabbos Kodesh are rewarded. He added that even those who eat *kugel* for their own pleasure will still receive reward for it!

Rabbi Itzik'l Pshevorsk *zt"l* used to distribute *kugel* on Shabbos morning after *davening.* Naturally, the floor became dirty from it. Once, after dividing the *kugel*, the Rabbi called out, "Chassidishe yingelech... and you aren't catching any *kugel*?" The Yidden looked around in amazement, not seeing a scrap of *kugel* left on the table. Pointing to the floor, the Rabbi called out, "There are treasures on the ground! Why don't you pick them up?" The Rabbi didn't give up until all the trodden *kugel* was picked up from the floor![17]

1 Zohar HaKadosh. 2 Megilah daf 6. 3 Tanchuma. 4 Pisron Torah. 5 Megilah daf 6. 6 Minchas 44. 7 Megillah daf 6. 8 Ayil Todah. 9 Chizkuni, Yalkut Me'am Lo'ez, Oitzer Agados. 10 R' Avraham ben Ezra, Rabbeinu Bechai. 11 Megillah daf 6, Rashi. 12 Ralbag. 13 Rashi V'Zos HaBrachah. 14 Shulchan HaTohar 242. 15 Panim Me'irim. 16 Zemiros Le'eter Pesuro. 17 HaRav HaChassid Reb Chaim Yaakov Grinfeld.

Answer for Parshas Vayigash:
Question 1: What did Yosef want to hint at to Yaakov by sending the wagons?
Answer: The last thing they learned together was the laws of the *eglah arufah* (the heifer whose neck was broken).

SHEMOS פרשת שמות

Question of the Week:
1. What do you see in the picture that relates to the plagues that Hashem punished the Mitzrim with *middah k'neged middah* (tit for tat), and what are they?

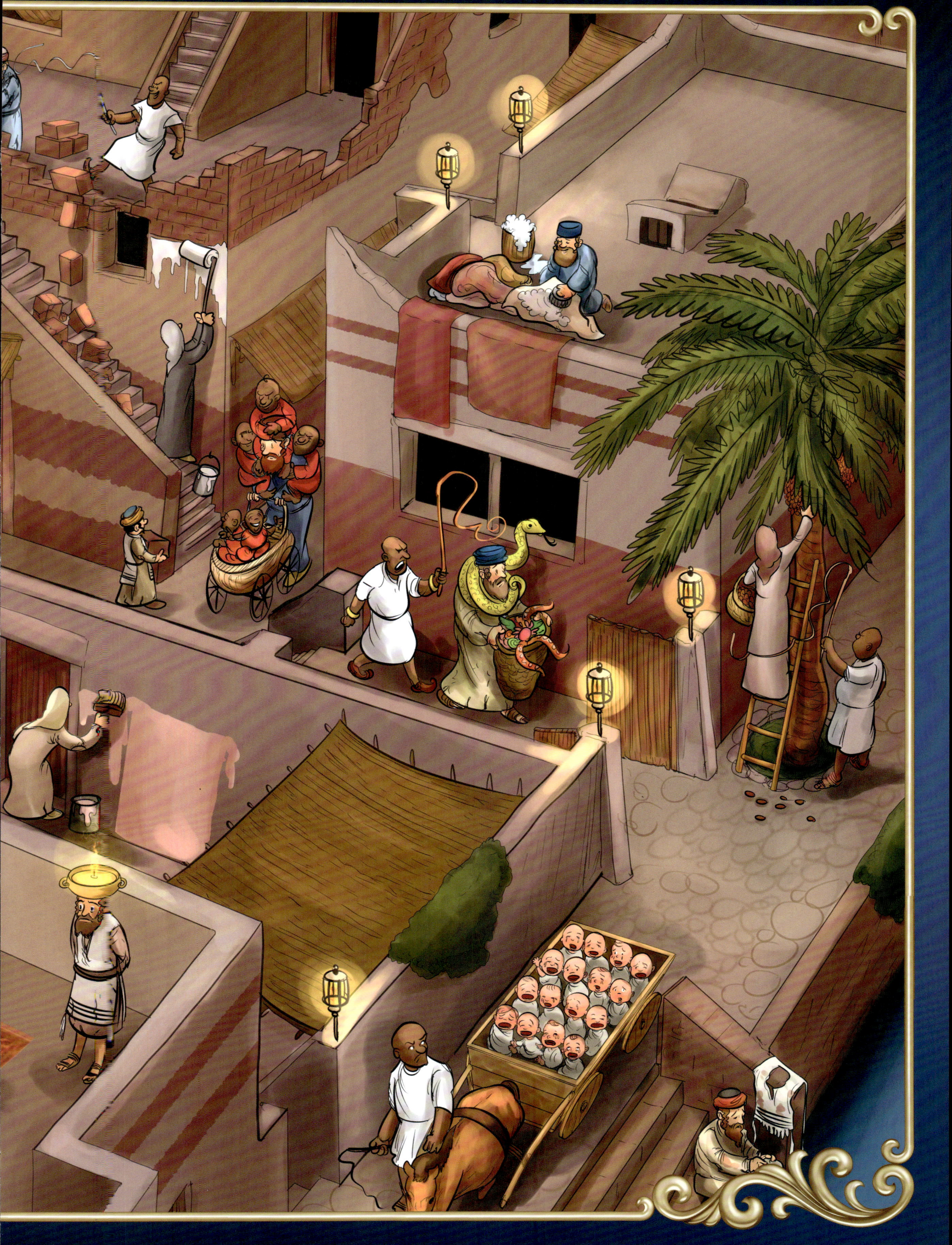

ויםררו את חייהם
They made their lives bitter

The Yidden were in Mitzrayim for 210 years. As long as Yosef was alive, they were treated with respect because of the family's relationship with the king.[1] In truth, some Yidden already started to feel some oppression right after Yaakov Avinu's death,[2] but as long as Yosef was still alive, the Mitzrim did not show this in public.[3]

The slavery began after Yosef's death. Little by little they began to enslave the Yidden more and more, until the death of Levi, the last of the Shevatim. This was ninety-four years after they had come down to Mitzrayim.[4]

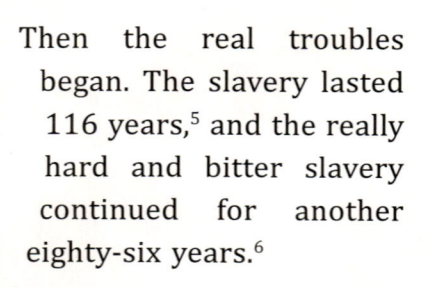

Then the real troubles began. The slavery lasted 116 years,[5] and the really hard and bitter slavery continued for another eighty-six years.[6]

Pharaoh made the Yidden's lives brutally miserable. He imposed on them very hard work that would wear them out and shatter their bodies. He forced the men to do women's work, and the women were given men's work.[7]

The Mitzrim went still a step further and ordered the Yidden to do useless work—work which made no sense and had no use—solely

> Pharaoh made the Yidden's lives brutally miserable. He imposed on them very hard work that would wear them out and break their bodies. He forced the men to do women's work, and the women were given men's work.

for the purpose of breaking them completely.[8] "Go and heat me up a pot of water!" the Mitzri ordered, and after the Yid went out, chopped the wood, heated the fire, boiled the water, and finally brought it to the Mitzri, the Mitzri would simply pour it out.[9] The Mitzrim also knocked down the buildings the Yidden had built.[10] The work of the Yidden had no purpose; it was only to humiliate and oppress them.[11]

The Yidden were enslaved for twenty-four hours a day.[12] During the day, they had to work hard physically to build the cities Pisom and Ramses, and then at night, when the hard work was finally over, every Mitzri had the right to hire them and order them to do any kind of work they fancied.[13] Then, as soon as the rooster crowed, the supervisors cruelly dragged the Yidden back to work.[14] They had to work with superhuman strength until late at night.[15] They had to start the work from scratch, kneading clay, making bricks, putting them in the buildings,[16] dragging up huge heavy stones, with the fear that they would slip down at any moment, and then they would be forced to climb up once again. All this as well as receiving a few good beatings on the way.[17]

Even the children were enslaved by the Mitzrim and had to work incredibly hard.[18]

When a Yid thought he might manage to go home to rest a little bit, a Mitzri would come and order him to plow, sow, harvest fruit from the field, chop wood, and draw water. The Mitzri used him all night, until the morning came and he was once again dragged back to work.[19] At night, again, when the Yid was hungry and exhausted, the Mitzri would drag him to his house, where he was participating in a grand meal. Although the Yid was completely starved, he was not allowed to touch a morsel. The Mitzri would place a lit candle on the Yid's head and position him in a space where he would give light to the room. The Yid would be warned that if the candle fell, his head would be chopped off.[20]

The Mitzrim would also order them to bring all kinds of creatures—like snakes, lizards, frogs, etc.—for their sports. Besides the disgust this brought to the Yidden, it also put them in danger. When the Mitzrim ordered them to go into the forest to catch specific wild animals without any weapons, some would never return home alive, and those who did manage to come back, usually did so in a bitten, wounded, and crippled state.[21]

The Mitzrim went still a step further and ordered the Yidden to do useless work—work which made no sense and had no use—solely for the purpose of breaking them completely. "Go and heat me up a pot of water!" the Mitzri ordered, and after the Yid went out, chopped the wood, heated the fire, boiled the water, and finally brought it to the Mitzri, the Mitzri would simply pour it out.

In addition, Pharaoh ordered their babies to be taken away.

The troubles, sufferings, and injuries the Yidden suffered in Mitzrayim led to them being completely broken in body when they finally left. Most of them were injured, blind, deaf, or lame.[22] It was a great miracle that the Yidden managed to survive the terrible troubles and tortures of the Mitzrim.[23]

---

1 Or HaChaim HaKadosh. 2 Rashi Bereishis 47:28, Malbim. 3 MeTamei HaShulchan. 4 Shemos Rabbah 1:4. 5 Yalkut Shimoni. 6 Seder Olam Rabbah. 7 Shemos Rabbah 1:11. 8 Midrash HaGadol. 9 Rashi Vayikra 25:43, Ha Emek Dever. 10 Midrash. 11 Midrash HaGadol, Malbim, Ha'Emek Dever. 12 Malbim, Or Maspik. 13 Ramban. 14 Midrash HaGadol, Midrash Lekach Tov, Rabbeinu Bechai. 15 Zohar HaKadosh. 16 Midrash Sechel Tov. 17 Pirkei d'Rabbi Eliezer, Abarbanel. 18 Pirkei d'Rabbi Eliezer. 19 Midrash Tanchuma, Shemos Rabbah, Rashbam. 20 Midrash Tanchuma, Pirkei d'Rabbi Eliezer, Shemos Rabbah. 21 Midrash Lekach Tov, Midrash HaGadol. 22 Bamidbar Rabbah 7:1. 23 Or Yisrael.

Answer for Parshas Vayechi:
Question: How many times do we find in the *parshah* that the Shechinah left Yaakov Avinu?
Answer: Twice (once when he wanted to *bentch* Ephraim and Menashe, and then when he wanted to *bentch* his children, the Shevatim).

פרשת וארא VA'EIRA

Question of the Week:
1. How did Hashem make fun of the Mitzrim with the plague of the frogs?

בוש

ותעל הצפרדע
And the frog(s) came up

The second plague was frogs. A huge frog came out of the river, opened its mouth, and spat out thousands of frogs at once.[1] When the Mitzrim wanted to try to get rid of the huge frog by hitting it, it just spat out more frogs with each blow.[2] At the same time, it produced a very strange high-pitched noise. In answer to this shout, thousands of frogs appeared from all around.[3]

It is said that it was not the frog that shouted, but it was the *malach* in charge of all the frogs who made the scream, calling all the frogs to gather together and attack Mitzrayim.[4]

Many frogs were created from each and every drop of water that fell on the earth[5]. Simultaneously, from every drop of sweat that the Mitzrim sweated, more frogs were created.[6] When anyone filled up a cup of water to drink, the whole cup was filled with frogs.[7] The frogs filled the whole country of Mitzrayim. People were literally unable to walk;[8] they just sank down in between all the frogs.[9] Those who would not give in, and were determined to get through, slipped and were badly injured.[10]

The frogs were able to walk through metal doors and walls,[11] into the dough, into the food, and even into the lit ovens, straight into the fire!

They crawled into the Mitzrim through their mouths, and once inside, they shouted loudly,[12] so that no one could speak to or hear each other.[13] No one could even sleep due to this plague,[14] and the smell was completely unbearable.[15]

However, the Yidden were not affected by the plague whatsoever. On the contrary, as soon as a Yid passed by, the frogs simply ran away.[16]

It is interesting to mention a dispute between the great Rishonim and Acharonim about the plague of frogs. We usually assume that the plague consisted of the small reptile that we know today as the frog, but Rabbeinu Chananal[17] and other Rishonim[18] believe that *tzefardeia* means the fearful and deadly crocodile.

The Abarbanel provides additional proof for this. We find that the *passuk* uses the word "נגף"[19] and "השחתה"[20] when it speaks of the plague of frogs. These words are only used for a deadly plague,[21] and the little frogs we know of today do not kill. Rabbi Sadia Gaon also brings the same opinion. In fact, we already find in Chazal that crocodiles came together with snakes in the plague of *tzefardeia*.[22]

Rashi[23] and Ibn Ezra,[24] however, believe that the plague was indeed the same frogs that we are familiar with today, and that the plague was not really fatal, but it definitely caused the Mitzrim a lot of unbearable pain and sorrow.[25]

Rabbi Eliezer Ashkenazi writes: "I claim that the Abarbanel had never seen a crocodile. If he had seen one, he would never have said this. I wonder how it is possible for a crocodile to enter the houses and the ovens and the dough?"[26]

This is what the Shavili group also ask, and they add, "If it *does* mean the crocodile, how is it possible, when such deadly and harmful creatures invaded the land, that there were Mitzrim left alive after the plague?"

Apparently, however, the same question could be asked after the plague of *arov* (wild animals).

The Mashgiach Rabbi Yechezkel Levenstein *zt"l* comes up with an interesting thought. As we know, Hashem is full of mercy, and even at the time of anger when He brought the terrible plagues on the Mitzrim, it was mixed with a measure of mercy, and Hashem took care that not all the Mitzrim would perish.[27]

The Malbim makes a compromise and says that it was both: the crocodiles killed, and the frogs got into the food and ovens, etc.[28]

An interesting thing happened during the plague of frogs. The Mitzrim were waging a war with their neighbors, the Kushites, regarding the position of the border between the two countries. The plague of frogs, which the *passuk* says was only in Mitzrayim, did not go beyond the border. This was the proof the Kushites needed. Everyone could see exactly how far the border of Mitzrayim went. The conflict was now settled, and the war ended.[29]

> Many frogs were created from each and every drop of water that fell on the earth. Simultaneously, from every drop of sweat that the Mitzrim sweated, more frogs were created. When anyone filled up a cup of water to drink, the whole cup was filled with frogs. The frogs filled the whole country of Mitzrayim. People were literally unable to walk; they just sank down in between all the frogs. Those who would not give in, and were determined to get through, slipped and were badly injured.

1 Shemos Rabbah 10:4. 2 Midrash HaGadol. 3 Sanhedrin 67, Tanna Devei Eliyahu. 4 Alshich HaKadosh. 5 Shemos Rabbah 10:3. 6 Zohar HaKadosh, Sefer HaYashar. 7 Tanchuma, Midrash Rabbah. 8 Rabbeinu Ephraim. 9 Midrash BeChidush. 10 Rabbeinu Ephraim. 11 Shemos Rabbah, Yalkut Shemoni 183. 12 Zohar HaKadosh, Shemos Rabbah. 13 Zohar HaKadosh. 14 Sechel Tov. 15 Midrash Lekach Tov. 16 Midrash Rabbah Naso 89. 17 Ramban Shemos 10:19. 18 Ibn Ezra 5:29, R' Y. Ibn Shu'ib. 19 Shemos 7:27. 20 Tehillim 78:48. 21 Bereishis 6:13. 22 Mishnas R' Eliezer, Baal HaTurim. 23 Shemos 7:27. 24 Shemos 8:29. 25 Maskil LeDavid. 26 Ma'asei Hashem 11. 27 Or Yechezkel 3:222. 28 Shemos 7:27. 29 Shemos Rabbah 10:2.

Answer for Parshas Shemos:
Question: What do you see in the picture that relates to the plagues that Hashem punished the Mitzrim with *middah k'neged middah* (tit for tat), and what are they?
Answer: Spilt Yiddishe blood (*dam*); ordered to catch frogs (*tzefardeia*); ordered to catch wild animals (*arov*); used in order to give light (*choshech*).

פרשת בא BO

Question of the Week:
1. When and where did Moshe Rabbeinu receive the prophecy of the plague of the death of the firstborn?

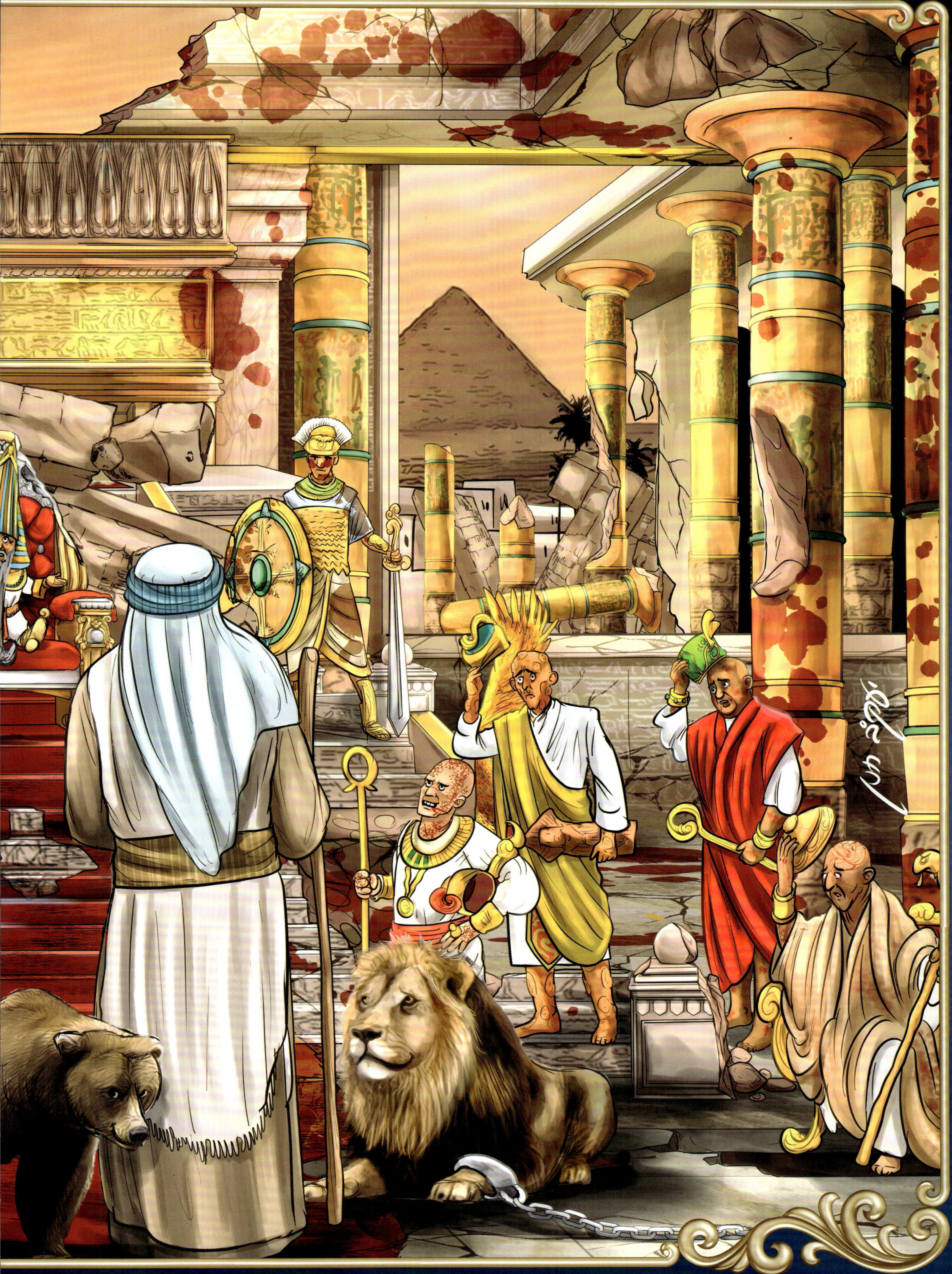

ויצא מעם פרעה בחרי אף
And he went out from Pharoah in burning anger

By the end of the month of Adar,[1] nine painful months had passed for the Mitzrim.[2] They were still suffering from the after-effects of the plague of darkness.

The plague of darkness was the most difficult of all the nine plagues.[3] This plague was not only a physical one, but also a psychological one, from which every Mitzri suffered greatly.[4]

Suddenly, without any warning,[5] it became dark for the Mitzrim. A thick darkness, which could be physically felt.[6] All lights were extinguished.[7] They could not see each other. They could not even see their hand if they put it in front of their face.[8]

"What happened?" the Mitzrim screamed hysterically. "What is going on? How much time has passed? How long will this go on?" The panic was very strong, and the anxiety grew from minute to minute. Hashem had to perform a miracle for the Mitzrim to survive, because they could not breathe at all during this plague.[9]

After three days it became even worse. They were suddenly unable to move.[10] Everyone stayed in exactly the same position he was in, as if he had been paralyzed.[11] Pharaoh became really frightened and wanted to call Moshe and tell him to send the Yidden out, but he could not move.[12]

> Suddenly, without any warning, it became dark for the Mitzrim. A thick darkness, which could be physically felt. All lights were extinguished. They could not see each other. They could not even see their hand if they put it in front of their face.

As soon as the plague ended, Pharaoh sent for Moshe. As usual Moshe entered the palace accompanied by a whole entourage of wild animals.[13] Pharaoh had 400 gates around the palace, and at each gate there were wild animals waiting to tear to pieces anyone who dared to pass through without permission. But when Moshe and Aharon came, the animals broke free from their chains and accompanied them into the palace, caressing them in a friendly manner. Everyone was struck with fear when they saw them entering the palace accompanied by such an army, and they took off their hats in respect.[14]

The palace had been increasingly destroyed by each plague. Each plague had left a lasting impression.[15] The palace walls were still dripping with the blood that had appeared during the plague of blood,[16] the ministers were still full of blisters,[17] and the palace itself was cracked and partially demolished by the hail that had destroyed everything.[18]

As usual, when Moshe and Aharon came, Pharaoh was sitting paralyzed on his throne[19]. Pharaoh was tiny, only a cubit high, and had a beard a cubit long, which trailed on the ground. His hat was also a cubit high. It appeared as if he was talking from the middle of his stomach. Compared to Moshe and Aharon, who were ten times taller than Pharaoh,[20] he was a sorry sight to see.[21]

Pharaoh said to Moshe, "I give the Yidden permission to leave, but your sheep and cattle must stay."

Moshe Rabbeinu disagreed. "They will all leave, together with the animals."

Pharaoh withdrew his words. "No one will leave!"

He was looking for a way to get rid of Moshe, when one of the magician advisors called out, "I noticed that the course of the plagues works as follows: two plagues with a warning and a third plague without any warning.

"As we have now ended the plague of darkness, which came without any warning, the next plague will come with a warning. Therefore, the King should order that Moshe may not appear before him. As long as he will not be able to warn you, there will not be another plague."[22]

"Don't you dare come to see my face again!" Pharaoh thundered at Moshe. "If so, I will kill you

As usual, when Moshe and Aaron came, Pharaoh was sitting paralyzed on his throne. Pharaoh was tiny, only a cubit high, and had a beard a cubit long, which trailed on the ground. His hat was also cubit high. It appeared as if he was talking from the middle of his stomach. Compared to Moshe and Aaron, who were ten times taller than Pharaoh, he was a sorry sight to see.

as a rebel!"[23]

"You know very well," said Moshe, "that you can do nothing more than talk,[24] but if you want it this way, let it be this way. I won't come to you anymore. Instead I will warn you now about the next plague."

Moshe Rabbeinu informed Pharaoh of the prophecy regarding the plague of the death of the firstborn. "If you don't want to see my face again, that's fine, but you should know that in the end you, together with your servants, will come and bow down to me, and beg us to leave."[25] Moshe Rabbeinu hit Pharaoh on his face and angrily left the palace.[26]

1 Sechel Tov. 2 Tanchuma. 3 Gur Ariah. 4 MeTamei HaShulchan. 5 Da'as Zekeinim. 6 Tanchuma. 7 Midrash Lekach Tov, Sforno, Ramban. 8 Ha'Emek Dever, Sefer HaYashar. 9 Yalkut Me'am Loez in the name of Ralbag. 10 Rashi. 11 Shemos Rabbah. 12 Avraham ben Ezra, Or HaChaim HaKadosh. 13 Noam Megadim from R' Eliezer Horowitz in the name of R' Yaakov Balig. 14 Midrash Yalkut. 15 Tiferes Tzion. 16 Midrash HaGadol. 17 Pirkei d'Rabbi Eliezer. 18 R' Yosef Bechor Shor. 19 Shemos Rabbah. 20 Marshu Moed Katan 18. 21 Shemos Rabbah, Rashi end of Chukas. 22 Or HaChaim HaKadosh. 23 Ibn Ezra. 24 Or HaChaim HaKadosh, Rav Peninim. 25 Shemos Rabbah. 26 Zevachim 102.

Answer for Parshas Va'eira:
Question: How did Hashem make fun of the Mitzrim with the plague of the frogs?
Answer: Pharaoh and the Mitzrim considered the River Nile as their god, and Hashem made fun of them by bringing the plague out from their river/god—and they were unable to do anything about it.

BESHALACH פרשת בשלח

?

Question of the Week:
1. Where is Megillas Esther hinted at in the *parshah*?

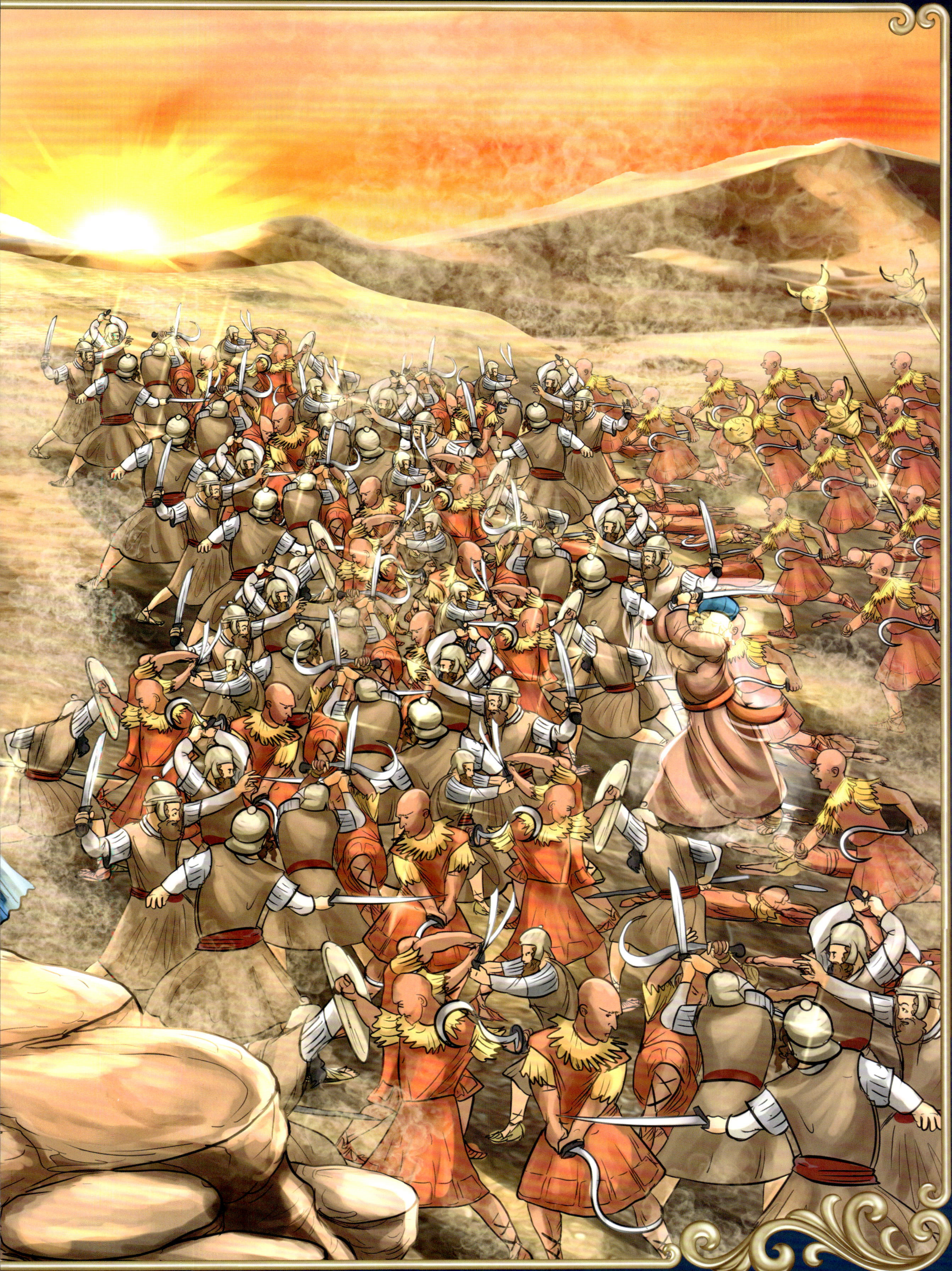

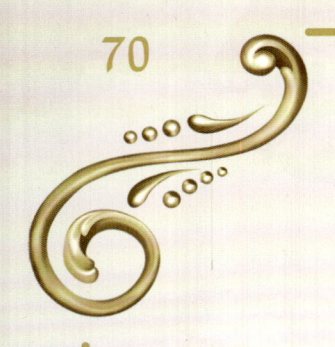

ויבא עמלק
And Amalek came

Rabbi Yochanan ben Nuri said, "After all the special wonders and miracles that Hashem performed for the Yidden in Mitzrayim and at the Yam Suf, the Yidden still asked, 'Is Hashem with us?'[1] Hashem answered, '*You* are testing *Me*. Let the wicked Amalek come and test *you*!'"[2]

This is similar to a parable about a child whose father took him on his shoulders and led him around the market. The son saw a beautiful object and said to the father, "Buy this object for me," and the father bought it for his son. This happened once, then a second time, and then a third.

Suddenly, the boy saw a man and called out to him, "Say, have you seen my father anywhere?"

The man answered him, "You fool! You are riding on your father's shoulders, and whatever you ask from him he is giving you, and you still ask if I've seen him?"

The father threw him off his shoulders, and a dog came and bit him.

It was the same when the Yidden came out of Mitzrayim. Hashem surrounded them with the special clouds to protect them. They asked for food, and Hashem brought them manna from heaven. Hashem provided them with all their needs, and they still asked, "Is Hashem with us?"

Hashem said, "Are you still doubting Me? I swear I will prove it to you! I will provoke the dog, the evil Amalek, on you!"[3]

Amalek marched 400 *parses* to come and fight with the Yidden.[4]

Why is he called Amalek (עמלק)? Because he came to lick up (ליקוק) the blood of the Yidden, like a dog.[5]

No enemy could do any harm to the Yidden because of the clouds of protection,[6] but Amalek made war with the Erev Rav who were camped outside, and killed many of them.[7] They also went to Mitzrayim and inquired about the names of the Shevatim. Then they stood outside the cloud and shouted to the Yidden, "Reuven, Shimon, Levi, come out, because I am your brother and I want to do business with you..." As soon as they were outside the protection of the cloud, Amalek killed them.[8] Then they shamed their bodies and blasphemed Hashem.[9]

Moshe Rabbeinu said to Yehoshua, "Choose important Yidden, *tzaddikim*, and go outside the cloud with them and wage war with Amalek.[10] Tomorrow I will fast.[11] I will go up to the top of the mountain and hold the staff of Hashem in my hand."[12]

Amalek chose soldiers whose birthday fell on that

day, because their *mazal* would be strong. Moshe went and changed the *mazalos*, so that Yehoshua would be able to defeat Amalek.[13] Moshe Rabbeinu also chose *tzaddikim* who were born in the month of Adar Sheini, as that month has no *mazal*; therefore, those who are born in that month are not bound by the *mazalos*.[14]

Moshe took the staff and spread his hands to the heaven and said, "Ribbono Shel Olam, with this staff, You brought the Yidden out of Mitzrayim and You split the sea for them. I beg of You, now do more miracles for them with it."[15]

When the Yidden came out of their tents, and when they saw how Moshe bowed to the ground, they did the same, and when they saw Moshe spread his hands to the heaven, they also spread their hands to the heaven and *davened* fervently for the success of the war.[16]

As long as Moshe had his hands spread upwards, Yehoshua prevailed over Amalek, but when Moshe

> It was the same when the Yidden came out of Mitzrayim. Hashem surrounded them with the special clouds to protect them. They asked for food, and Hashem brought them manna from heaven. Hashem provided them with all their needs, and they still asked, "Is Hashem with us?"

lowered his hands, Amalek was stronger. The reason for this was because as long as Moshe had his hands raised to the heaven, the Yidden turned to Hashem and believed in Him, and this helped Yehoshua in the war.[17]

Due to the sins of the Yidden, Moshe's hands became heavy,[18] and it was difficult for him to keep them up. He sat down on a stone, and Aharon and Chur put their hands under him as a support.

Could Moshe not sit on a cushion instead of a stone? But Moshe said, "As long as the Yidden are suffering, I will join with them and share their suffering."[19]

It was getting close to night, and the war had not yet ended. Moshe Rabbeinu kept the sun from setting until Yehoshua, with the help of Hashem, defeated the evil Amalek.[20]

1 Pirkei d'Rabbi Eliezer 44. 2 Shemos Rabbah 22. 3 Yalkut Shimoni Beshalach Remes 261. 4 Mechilta Rashbi 17:8. 5 Tanchuma Yashan Yisro 4. 6 Pirkei d'Rabbi Eliezer. 7 Rashi end of Ki Seitzei. 8 Tanchuma Yashan Ki Seitzei 13. 9 Pesikta Rabbasi 12. 10 Mechilta Beshalach. 11 Targum Yonasan 17-19. 12 Chizkuni. 13 Yerushalmi Rosh Hashanah 83. 14 Rabbeinu Ephraim. 15 Tanchuma Beshalach. 16 Pirkei d'Rabbi Eliezer 44. 17 Rosh Hashanah 3:8. 18 Pesikta Rabbasi 12. 19 Ta'anis 11. 20 Tanchuma Beshalach 28.

Answer to Parshas Bo:
Question: When and where did Moshe Rabbeinu receive the prophecy of the plague of the death of the firstborn?
Answer: While still in the palace, Hashem raised Moshe Rabbeinu, and then told him the prophecy.

פרשת יתרו · YISRO

Question of the Week:
1. Why did Hashem place the mountain over the Yidden? After all, they had already said "נעשה ונשמע".

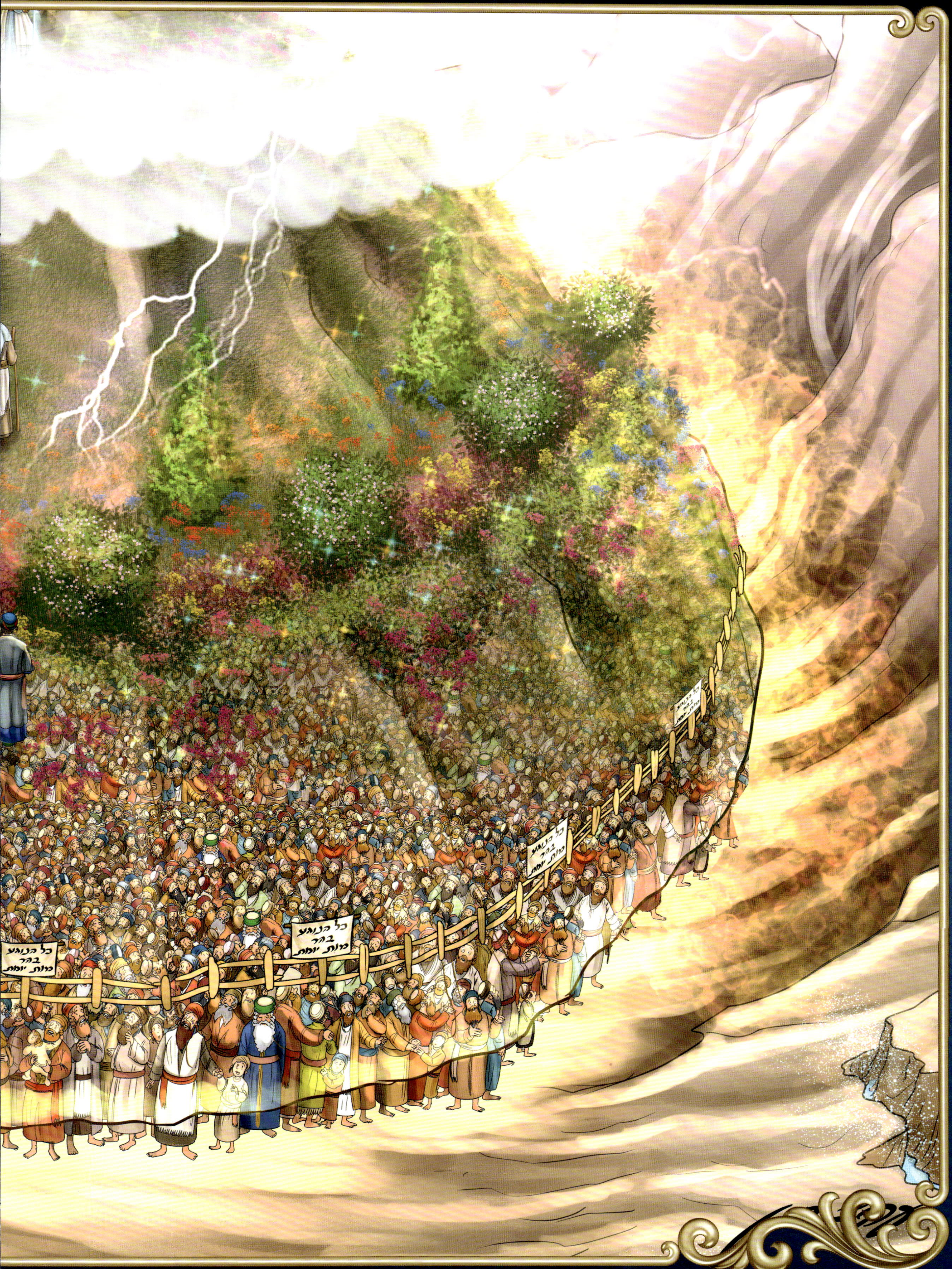
כל הנוגע
בהר
מות יומת

ויתיצבו בתחתית ההר

And they stood at the bottom of the mountain

Hashem asked all the nations, "Do you want to accept my Torah?" Each nation came up with a different excuse not to accept the Torah.[1]

Hashem then went, together with His *malachim*, to the Bnei Yisrael and asked them if they wanted the Torah. Their answer was, "נעשה ונשמע—We will do and listen to whatever Hashem commands!"

Hashem said, "I need guarantors who will guarantee that you will actually obey what is written in My Torah!"[2]

The Yidden answered, "The heaven and earth will be our guarantors."

Hashem said, "Heaven and earth do not last forever, and they will eventually be destroyed."[3]

The Yidden brought the little children, even the nursing babies in their cribs, and said, "These are our guarantors. They will guarantee that we will always guard Your Torah!"[4]

Hashem said, "These are really good guarantors! If you keep the Torah, it will be very good for you; but if not, I will hold your guarantors—the children—responsible!"[5]

All of a sudden, Har Sinai pulled itself out of the earth and lifted itself up into the air,[6] and Hashem placed it above the Yidden.[7] A hole was hollowed out under the mountain, and Hashem gathered all of Klal

The Yidden brought the little children, even the nursing babies in their cribs, and said, "These are our guarantors. They will guarantee that we will always guard Your Torah!"

Yisrael inside the hollow mountain. They were surrounded from all four sides and from above.[8]

The mountain became transparent like crystal,[9] and one could see exactly what was happening outside and inside.[10] It sparkled with a heavenly shine.[11]

Then the voice of Hashem thundered in the ears of all the Yidden: "If you accept the Torah, it will be good for you! But if not, you will be buried here under the mountain!"[12]

Then all the Yidden burst into tears, did *teshuvah* from the bottom of their hearts, and called out, "Everything that Hashem says, we will do and we will listen!"

Hashem then made the mountain like a *chuppah*[13] and sanctified the Bnei Yisrael with the Torah, like a *chassan* and *kallah*.[14] The *malachim* and *seraphim* stood at the *chuppah* and watched the love of Hashem to Klal Yisrael; the Zekeinim were like the witnesses at a *chuppah*; and Moshe was like the man who takes the cup of Kiddushin in his hand.[15]

The mountain (the *chuppah*) was surrounded by precious stones, pearls, and diamonds,[16] and it was magnificently adorned with grass and flowers.[17] The whole mountain was surrounded by fire,[18] and the flames of the fire reached up to the sky.[19]

The Yidden stood there barefoot because of the respect and great fear they had towards this holy place, similar to Moshe Rabbeinu at the Burning Bush.[20] A miracle happened, and the Bnei

Yisrael, who were under the mountain, rose in the air.[21] They floated and no longer touched the ground, as it was very holy due to the presence of the Shechinah.[22] At that same moment, other mountains also rose in the air, as if in a dance, and some mountains fled from their place out of fear, until Hashem calmed them down and they returned to their places.[23]

The mountain (the chuppah) was surrounded by precious stones, pearls, and diamonds, and it was magnificently adorned with grass and flowers. The whole mountain was surrounded by fire, and the flames of the fire reached up to the sky.

The whole world trembled and waited to see whether the Yidden would accept the Torah or not.[24] The earth opened and the abyss came up and water gushed out from under the earth.[25]

Even though it was a clear day,[26] sounds of powerful thunder and lightning were suddenly heard,[27] which shook the world.[28]

The sound of a *shofar* was heard.[29] This became stronger and stronger,[30] until it was heard all over the world.[31] It was a great surprise because, since the world had been created, people had not heard the sound of a *shofar*.[32]

With the sound of the *shofar* came a resurrection,[33] and all the dead in the world rose up, alive, and stood on their feet to join the holy and fearful event of the Giving of the Torah.[34] The *malachim* and *seraphim* sang songs to Hashem.[35] Moshe Rabbeinu, who was blessed with a beautiful voice and could sing very sweetly,[36] also sang *shirah*,[37] and all the kings around the world sang praises to Hashem.[38]

1 Midrash Aseres HaDibros, Midrash Tenaim, Pirkei d'Rabbi Eliezer, Mechilta. 2 Mechilta d'Rashbi. 3 Midrash Mishlei 86. 4 Midrash Tehillim, Midrash Aseres HaDibros. 5 Midrash Mishlei. 6 Shir HaShirim 8:2. 7 Shabbos 88. 8 Marshu. 9 Targum Yonasan ben Uziel. 10 Ahavas Yonasan. 11 Targum Yonasan ben Uziel. 12 Mechilta d'Rashbi. 13 Nachal Kadumim Devarim. 14 Shita MeKubetzes Kesubos 7. 15 Midrash Hashkem, brought from Menoras HaMe'or. 16 Machzor Vitri Shavuos. 17 Lavush 494. 18 Kuzari. 19 Devorim 4:11, Mechilta, Ramban, Rabbeinu Bechai. 20 Tosfos HaShalem Shemos 3:5. 21 Markeves HaMishnah. 22 Rabbeinu Bechai. 23 Zohar HaKadosh. 24 Shabbos 88. 25 Bereishis Rabbah 33, Vayikra Rabbah 27. 26 Tosefta. 27 Piyut second day of Shavuos. 28 Zevuchim 116. 29 Midrash HaGadol. 30 Shemos 19. 31 Pesikte Chadete. 32 Avraham ben Ezra. 33 Zohar HaKadosh. 34 Pirkei d'Rabbi Eliezer. 35 Nusach HaTana'im that one reads on Shavuos. 36 Ramban Siso, Shalsheles HaKabbalah. 37 Erchin 11, Machzor Vitri. 38 Zevuchim.

Answer for Parshas Beshalach:
Question: Where is Megillas Esther hinted at in the *parshah*?
Answer: From the *passuk* describing the Battle of Amalek, the Gemara learns that the Megillah of Purim should be written.

MISHPATIM פרשת משפטים

Question of the Week:
1. In what way is a person free from paying if he damaged something while he was asleep?

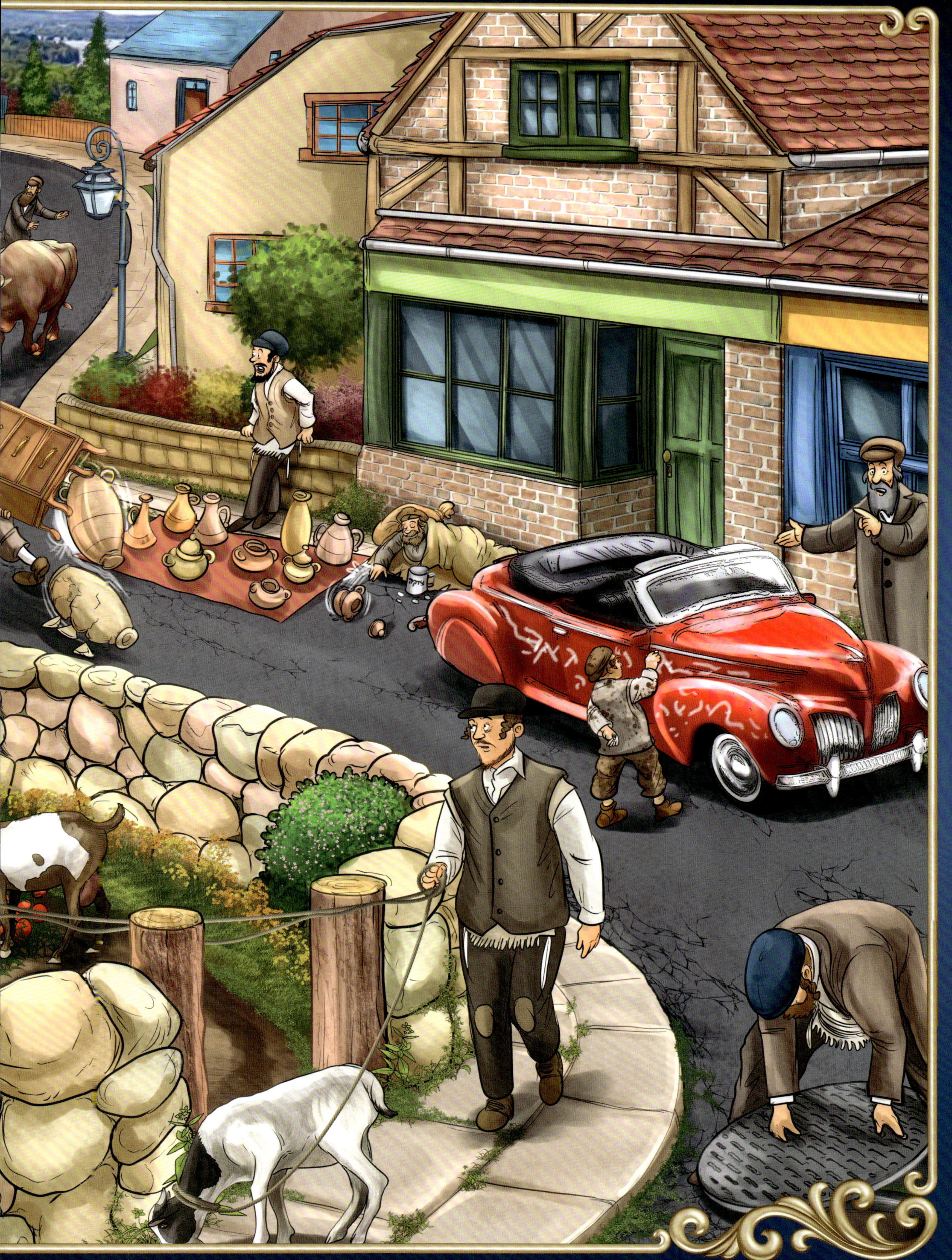

ארבעה אבות נזיקין
Four categories of damages

Besides the fact that it is forbidden for one person to harm another, the Torah requires that a person should watch over his animals so that they do not harm anyone, or another's possessions.[1]

The law is a reasonable one that everyone can understand. If there were no laws in the world, the world would not be able to exist.[2] Rabbi Yonah states that the prohibition is derived from "לא תגזול—*You should not steal.*"[3] The Rosh writes that it is taken from the *passuk* "דרכיה דרכי נועם וכל נתיבותיה שלום—*The way of the Torah is pleasant and all its paths are peace*," meaning that one should behave nicely towards one another.[4]

A person is obliged to watch over his animals with a firm guard so that they are not able to cause any damage to another person.[5] If one's animal *did* cause damage to another person, the owner of the animal has to pay for the damage to the injured party.

There are four main things that a person is obliged

A person is obliged to watch over his animals with a firm guard so that they are not able to cause any damage to another person. If one's animal did cause damage to another person, the owner of the animal has to pay for the damage to the injured party.

to take care of so that neither he nor his animal harms anyone. The first is שור המזיק, which means that he must prevent his ox from harming someone else. The second is בור, which means that a person must not dig or open a pit in a place where people walk (public grounds), as this can cause someone to fall in and get hurt. The third is מבעה. This is called שן המזיק, which means that he must make sure his animals do not eat anything from another's field. The fourth is הבער, which means that he must take care that a fire he has lit does not burn or damage another's property.

There is a dispute in the Gemara about the third thing, מבעה. Rav believes that this applies to אדם המזיק, which means that a person must take care that he himself does not harm another person.[6]

If a person or his animal has caused damage to another person, he is obliged to pay.

There are two ways of payment: 1) נזק שלם, which means that he must pay the entire value of the damage; and 2) חצי נזק, which means that he has to pay only half of the damage, as follows:

The damage of an ox is divided into two. For the first three damages the ox executed, he is called a harmless ox—a "Tam"—and the owner is only obliged to pay for half of the damage: חצי נזק.

If the ox continues to harm for a fourth time, or more, he is already a harmful ox—a "Mued"—and the owner must pay full damage: נזק שלם.[7]

שור המזיק is divided into two separate ways of damaging:

1. With his horn
2. With his feet

When the ox continuously hurts in an unusual way—for example, it pushes a person or an animal—it is called damaging with its horn, and the *dinim* of "Tam" and "Mued" are applied.

When it harms in an ordinary way—for example, it walks on the road and while walking it steps on some food—it is called damaging with its feet, and only the *din* of "Mued" applies, always paying for the full damage: נזק שלם.

שן המזיק means that when the animal eats fruits, etc. from someone else's field, the owner always pays only half the damage: חצי נזק. This would not apply if the ox damaged in an unusual way; for example, when it eats clothes or dishes, which is definitely not the norm, then the difference between "Tam" and "Mued" applies, and only on the third occasion do you pay full damage: נזק שלם. The Mishnah says: "חרש שוטה וקטן פגיעתן רע, הם שחבלו באחרים פטורים ואחרים שחבלו בהם חייבים"—Whoever is harmed by a deaf mute, a fool, or a child, has done badly, because if they harm you, they are exempt from paying, but *the one who harms them must pay for the damage*."[8] This means that a father is not obligated to pay when his child harms someone. The child is not obligated to pay even when he grows up and becomes an adult, because when he did the damage he was not responsible. But the Ari HaKadosh states that the child *does* need to pay when he is an adult, and he must do proper *teshuvah*.[9]

If a person has taken good care of his animal and yet it has caused damage, the owner is exempt from paying, because he did what he could.

This only applies if his *animal* caused damage, but if *he himself* causes damage, it is not so. For a person, they say, "אדם מועד לעולם בין שוגג בין מזיד בין ער בין ישן—*A person is always responsible never to harm, and even if he harms unwillingly, or in the middle of sleep, he always needs to pay*."[10] A human being has sense and can protect himself from harming someone else.

---

1 Rambam Nezikei Mamon 85. 2 Chinach Mitzvah 49. 3 Rabbeinu Yona Avos 81. 4 Techuves HaRoch 108:10. 5 Bava Kama 81:41. 6 Bava Kama daf 3. 7 Bava Kama 81:4. 8 Bava Kama 87. 9 Sha'ar HaGilgulim in name of the Ari HaKadosh. 10 Bava Kama 82:46.

Answer to Parshas Yisro:
Question: Why did Hashem place the mountain over the Yidden? After all, they had already said "נעשה ונשמע".
Answer: They only said "We will do and we will hear" regarding תורה שבכתב (the Written Torah) but not regarding תורה שבעל פה (the Oral Torah).

פרשת תרומה TERUMAH

Question of the Week:
1. How was the middle beam inserted into the walls of the Mishkan?

באר שבע

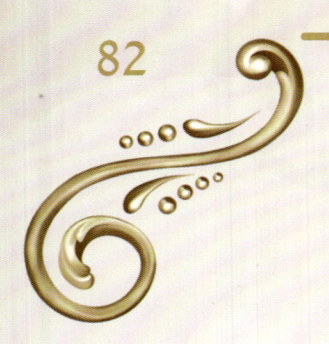

אמר רבי תנחומא
Rabbi Tanchuma says

"Ai, ai, ai... Rashi asks..." the rebbe sings with gusto in the classroom, while all the children are listening with interest and diligently following in the Chumash. "ומנין היו להם עצים במדבר— *From where did they get wood in the desert?* You hear, children," the rebbe explains with enthusiasm, "Hashem asked the Yidden to build a Mishkan for him in the desert, a holy tent where the Shechinah would rest among them.

"It was necessary to build the main part of the Mishkan with wood. And later, in order to keep the walls together, they needed one long narrow piece of wood (the middle beam) of seventy-two cubits long[1] that ran through it all! Miraculously, this wood managed to turn itself round all three corners, connecting all the walls together.[2]

"So the question arises—and this is what Rashi HaKadosh asks—where did they get wood in the desert? Does anything grow in the desert? Of course not! The desert is barren and desolate, and nothing grows there. If so, where did the Yidden get wood to build the Mishkan?

"Answers Rashi," the rebbe continues the song, "Rabbi Tanchuma said, dear children..." The rebbe pauses in the middle of teaching the Rashi. "Rashi brings an answer to this question from Rabbi Tanchuma, but in an abbreviated form. Let me first explain the story with all the details as it

So the question arises—and this is what Rashi HaKadosh asks—where did they get wood in the desert? Does anything grow in the desert? Of course not! The desert is barren and desolate, and nothing grows in it. If so, where did the Yidden get wood to build the Mishkan?

Mitzrayim.[3]

"Yaakov Avinu had another reason for going to Beersheva on his way to Mitzrayim. From the time of Avraham Avinu, people knew that the Yidden would go into *galus*, as Hashem had told Avraham at the Bris Bein HaBesarim. Avraham Avinu knew that after the Yidden left the *galus*, they would need to build a tent for Hashem, and for this, very large, wide, long boards would be needed, especially the very long narrow beam of wood that would encompass all three walls of the Mishkan.

is explained in the Midrash, and then we will look inside the Rashi. Listen very carefully, my dear children.

"Before Yaakov Avinu went down to settle in Mitzrayim—at the request of his son Yosef HaTzaddik—he traveled to Beersheva. This was the same place that Yaakov had been years before to ask Hashem's permission before he went to Charan, to Lavan. Now he went there again, to ask Hashem if he should go to

"Knowing that in the desert the Yidden would not have any wood from which to make the boards, Avraham planted cedar trees in Beersheva—they grow tall and wide—so that in years to come, when the Yidden needed them, they would be able to use them. This knowledge was handed down from generation to generation until Yaakov Avinu.

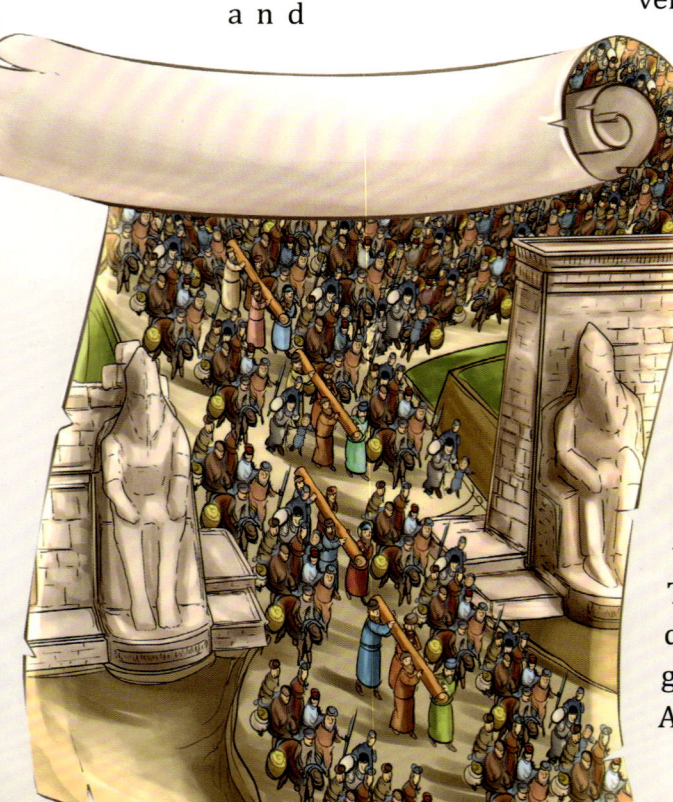

"Now, when Yaakov Avinu went down to Mitzrayim, he understood that this would be the beginning of the *galus*, and he therefore realised that the time had come to take the trees that his *zeide* Avraham had planted. This was the second reason Yaakov had for going to Beersheva first. He wanted to cut down all the trees that had grown since Avraham Avinu had planted them.

"He actually cut down all the trees and carried them down to Mitzrayim and planted them there, where they continued to grow for another 210 years, and when the Yidden left Mitzrayim, they cut them down. By now they were very large and long. They were loaded onto wagons and taken out of Mitzrayim and into the desert. And it was these trees that provided them with enough wood to make the boards to build the Mishkan.[4]

"Children, since Rashi is bringing down explanations from Rabbi Tanchuma," the rebbe said, "it would be interesting to know who Rabbi Tanchuma really was. So let me tell you a little bit about him.

"There were two Midrashim; one was called Midrash Tanchuma, and the other was called Midrash Yelamdenu. The *Seder HaDorot* states that

1 Rabbeinu Bechai. 2 Shabbos 98. 3 Ramban Bereishis 46:1. 4 Midrash Bereishis Rabbah 97:4.

> "Now, when Yaakov Avinu went down to Mitzrayim he understood that this would be the beginning of the *galus*, and he therefore realised that the time had come to take the trees that his *zeide* Avraham had planted. This was the second reason Yaakov had for going to Beersheva first. He wanted to cut down all the trees that had grown since Avraham Avinu had planted them.

both Midrashim are written by the same author—the Amora Rabbi Tanchuma bar Abba—and it was known as Midrash Yelamdenu because each *parshah* begins with the words 'Yelamdenu Rabbeinu.'

"The Chida, however, in his sefer *Shem HaGedolim* writes that they are two separate Midrashim by two separate authors, and that the Midrash Tanchuma we have today is not the original Midrash of Rabbi Tanchuma. He states that the Midrash Yelamdenu is actually the original Midrash of Rabbi Tanchuma, and we do not have the real Midrash Tanchuma.

"In fact, our Midrash Tanchuma consists of both; you can see the Midrashim of Midrash Yelamdenu at the beginning of each *parshah*, as well as the words of Chazal on the *parshah*.

"We can talk much more about this matter, perhaps on another occasion," the rebbe concluded.

Answer to Parshas Mishpatim:
Question: In what way is a person free from paying if he damaged something while he was sleep?
Answer: If, after he has already fallen asleep, an article was put in a place that caused him to damage it.

TETZAVEH פרשת תצוה

Question of the Week:
1. How much oil did they have to put in the *menorah* each day?

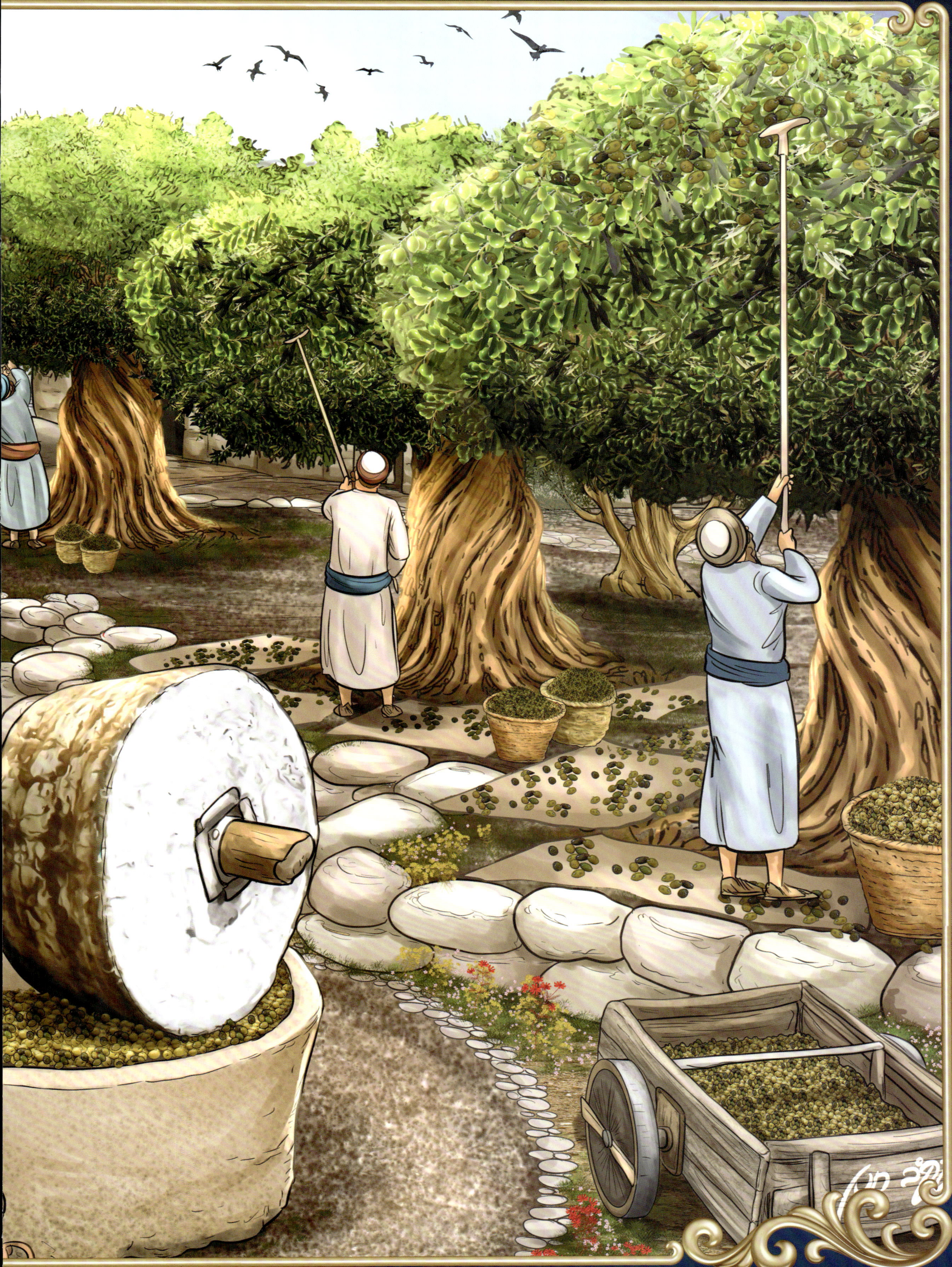

שמן זית זך כתית למאור
Pure, beaten olive oil for the light

Hashem told Moshe Rabbeinu to instruct Klal Yisrael to bring oil to light the *menorah*.

"The oil the Yidden should bring for the *menorah*," Hashem commanded, "must be very clear oil, without any residue, pounded in a pestle, and not ground in a grinder."[1]

There are three types of oil, which are divided into three—nine in total.

The olives on an olive tree are divided into three types.

1. The olives growing at the very top, which ripen differently. As we know, the sun shines in the morning in the east and travels around the earth until the evening, when it sets in the west. Accordingly, there is always sun at the top of the tree, because there is nothing there to block it, and since the sun shines on the top of the tree all day long, the olives at the top of the tree become completely ripe.

2. The olives in the middle of the tree, which do not get the heat of the sun all day—only when the sun shines on the side they are situated. This means that when the sun is on the east side, it shines on the east side of the tree—but no sun will shine on the west side of the tree, because the tree itself casts a shadow that blocks its rays. The olives that grow on the opposite side of the tree have the same problem. When the sun is closer to the west side in the afternoon, it shines on the west side of the tree, but not on the east side of the tree, because the tree blocks it from reaching the other side.

3. The olives that grow at the very bottom of the tree, which ripen the least because the sun hardly reaches there; the branches above block the sun.

It follows from this that there are three types of oil:

1. The oil that comes from the uppermost olives, which have been very well ripened. This oil is very juicy and good.

2. The oil that comes from the olives that grow in the middle of the tree. They are less ripe, so the oil from them is weaker.

3. The oil that comes from the olives that grow at the bottom the tree. These are the least ripe, so the oil from them is of very poor quality.

Each of the three oils is also divided into three different phases, depending on how the oil is extracted from the olives, as follows:

1. The first way to extract the oil is to put the olives in a basket and hit them until they split. The olives are not crushed, but only split. Then the split olives are placed in a basket with holes in the bottom, and the basket is placed in a bowl. The olives lie in the basket, and very clean, clear oil flows from them into the bowl below. This oil is very expensive, because there is very little of it.

2. The olives are then taken out of the basket, and they are put into a press with a net, and the press squeezes out the excess oil from the olives. This oil flows into a pit near the press. The oil that comes out of the press is no longer as pure, and contains a little residue.

3. There is still some oil left in the olives at this point. The crushed olives are now put into a mill and ground completely until the last remaining oil has been extracted. This oil, which comes out after grinding, contains a lot of residue.

The three phases of extracting oil are used with all three above-mentioned olives. Therefore, there are total of nine types of oil altogether: three types of oil from the olives at the top of the tree, three from the olives in the middle of the tree, and three from the olives at the bottom of the tree.

The Torah only allows the first type of oil from each of the types of olives to be used for the *menorah* because it is clear and pure—שמן זית זך.

However, for the *korban minchah*, which requires much more oil than the *menorah*, the Torah permits the use of all the types of oil, for monetary reasons.

Therefore, of the nine types of oil, three of them are kosher for the *menorah*, and the remaining six are kosher for the *korban minchah*.[2]

The olives are then taken out of the basket, and they are put into a press with a net, and the press squeezes out the excess oil from the olives. This oil flows into a pit near the press. The oil that comes out of the press is no longer as pure, and contains a little residue.

1 Shemos 27:20, Rashi. 2 Mishnah and Gemara Minchas 86, according to Peirush HaTosfos and Shitus Rabbanan.

Answer for Parshas Teruma:
Question: How was the middle beam inserted into the walls of the Mishkan?
Answer: It was pushed into a hole on one side, and it miraculously ran through all three walls.

Purim פורים

Question of the Week:
1. Who was Hasach?

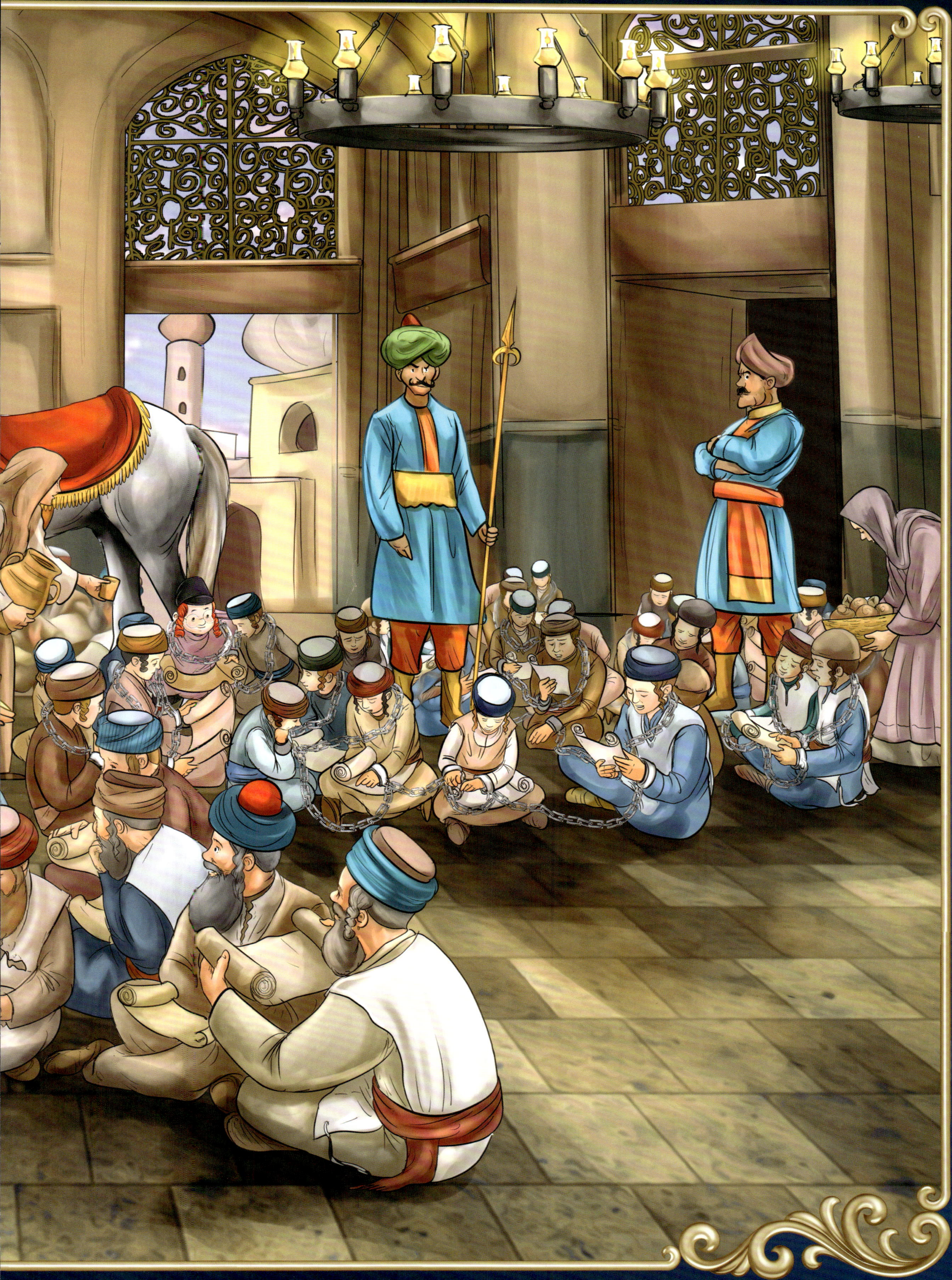

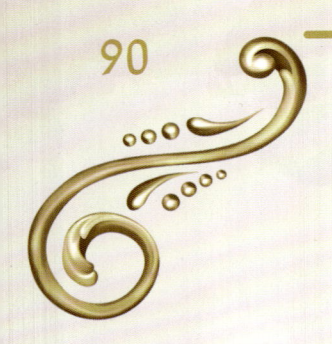

ככה יעשה לאיש
So shall be done to man

The horses ran with the king's command to kill all of Klal Yisrael, from big to small, young to old, men and women and children—and all on one day. A sadness descended upon the town of Shushan. On hearing the decree, Mordechai HaTzaddik immediately tore his clothes, dressed in sackcloth, put ashes on his forehead, and ran through the streets of Shushan crying a bitter cry at the terrible decree.

Esther was preparing for the Yom Tov of Pesach and knew nothing of the decree until her servants came to tell her. "Mordechai is running through the streets dressed in sackcloth and shouting and crying!"

"Hasach," Esther called, "go and see what's going on with Mordechai, and give him fresh clothes to change into."

Mordechai did not accept the clothes and instead begged Esther to put her life in danger for the sake of her people and go and beg the king to cancel Haman's decree.

Even though going to the king without being invited would put her life in danger, Esther still went, announcing beforehand that Mordechai should proclaim a three-day fast. Mordechai listened to Esther's request and immediately sent a message throughout all of Shushan telling the people to fast. The message was proclaimed loudly. Mordechai himself went from street to street demanding that everyone, from big to small, should participate in the fast.

Mordechai HaTzaddik gathered all the children of Shushan in the shul and prevented them from eating or drinking. He dressed them in sackcloth and put ashes on them and ordered them: "Shout loudly and cry to Hashem in heaven to annul the wicked decree!"

On the third day of the fast, Esther rose from her ashes, put on her royal clothes, and went to the king, thus putting her life in danger. Hashem made her find favor in the eyes of the king, and the king stretched out his golden staff to her, asking, "What is it, my dear Esther? Tell me what you want, and I will give you everything, up to half my kingdom!"

"I don't want anything," Esther replied, "only for the king to come together with Master Haman for a feast."

That night, after the feast, Achashverosh could not sleep, so his servant read to him. He read about when Mordechai had saved the king from death. Just at that moment, Haman arrived to tell him that Mordechai should be hanged. Achashverosh did not want to hear anything, though, and simply asked, "What should be done to someone to whom the king wants to give a reward?"

Haman, who was sure the king had only *him* in mind, immediately replied, "The king should command that the purple robe he wore on his coronation be put on that man, together with the royal crown. Put him on the king's own royal horse and lead him round Shushan, calling out 'This is what is done for someone whom the king wishes to honor!'"

"Very good, Haman!" Achashverosh laughed. "Go to Mordechai the Jew and do with him exactly as you just said!"

Haman felt like he could not breathe. His face turned pale, his eyes darkened, his lips parted, his thoughts turned into confusion in his head, and his knees knocked together in great fear. He argued with the king, but after realizing that the matter had been finalized, he had no choice but to do as the king had ordered.

With a bowed head, like a mourner, he entered the king's treasure chamber and took out the king's clothes, then he collected the king's horse from the royal stables, and he himself went to Mordechai.

Someone approached Mordechai and said, "Why are you sitting here? Haman is on his way, and he wants to hang you on the gallows he has prepared for you."

Mordechai immediately divided the shul: his pupils with the sages on one side, and the little children on the other. They all started to cry and object about what was going to happen to Mordechai, their leader... but Hashem, who had been listening to their *tefillos* for a long time, had very different plans for Mordechai HaTzaddik.

Mordechai HaTzaddik was standing at the side *davening* to Hashem when Haman entered with the prescribed clothing. When he saw that Mordechai was busy *davening*, he waited patiently. He sat down among the students of Mordechai and asked

Even though going to the king without being invited would put her life in danger, Esther still went, announcing beforehand that Mordechai should proclaim a three-day fast. Mordechai listened to Esther's request and immediately sent a message throughout all of Shushan telling the people to fast. The message was proclaimed loudly, Mordechai himself went from street to street demanding that everyone, from big to small, should participate in the fast.

them, "What are you doing now?"

They said, "Today is the Yom Tov of Pesach, and this is when the *korban omer* was brought when the Beis HaMikdash stood."

"And what did the *omer* consist of?" Haman was curious. "Silver or gold?"

"Neither," answered the students. "It consisted of plain, simple barley."

"How much was the *omer* worth? Twenty *kikar*? Ten *kikar*?"

"No, my dear Haman," they laughed, "it was not worth more than ten *me'ah*."

"Woe is to me!" Haman lamented. "Your ten *me'ah* pushed away my 10,000 silver *kikar* that I gave to the king!"

Haman then led Mordechai through the streets of Shushan and called out:

"ככה יעשה לאיש אשר המלך חפץ ביקרו—This is what is done for someone whom the king wishes to honor."[1]

1 Sefer Hanifla Pirsomei Nisa.

Answer to Parshas Tetzave:
Question: How much oil did they have to put in the *menorah* each day?
Answer: Half a *lug*. There had to be enough for the long nights in the month of Teves.

פרשת כי תשא KI SISA

Question of the Week:
1. How many times were the Yidden counted in the desert?

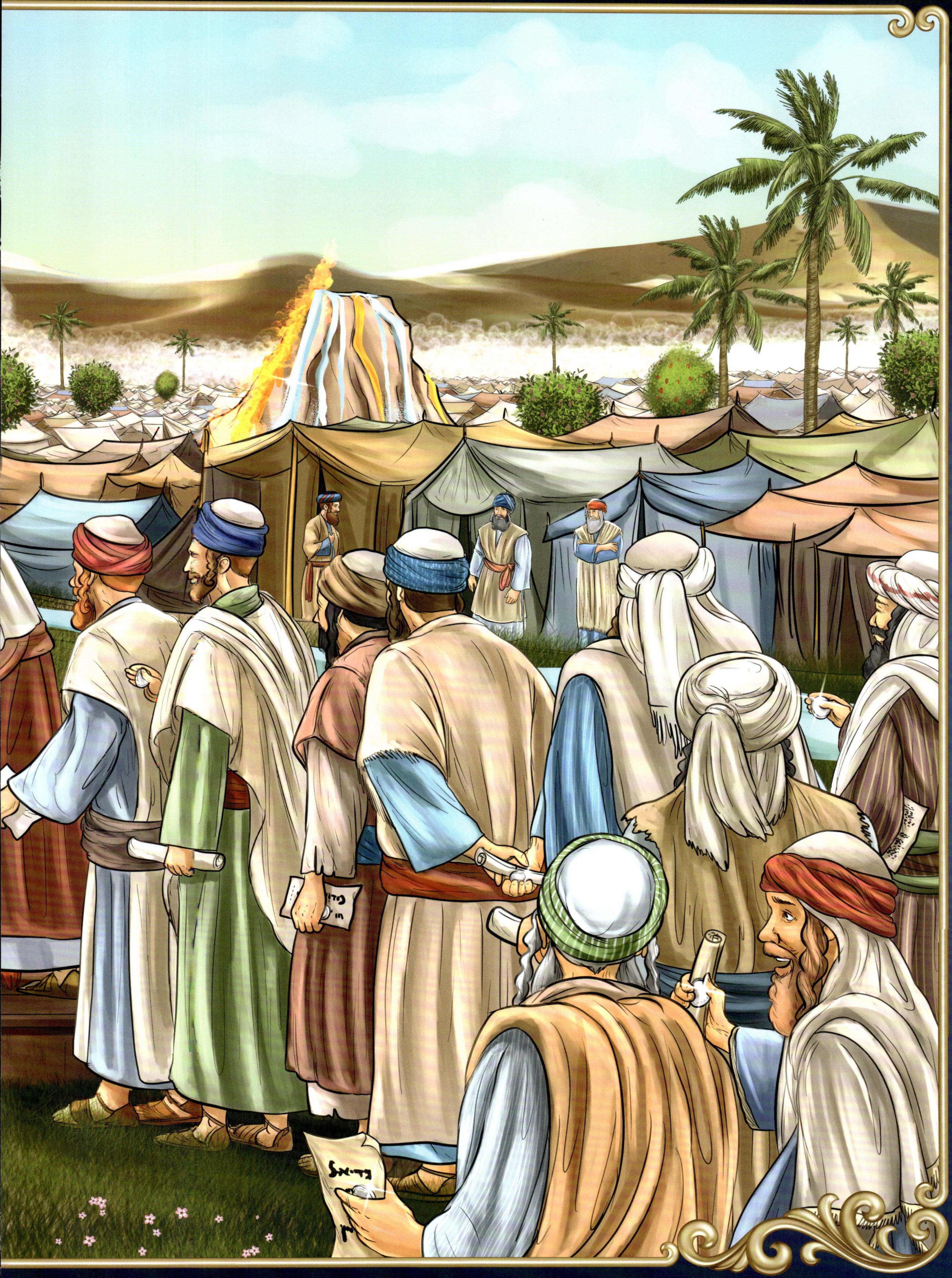

תשא את ראש בני ישראל
Count the heads of the Bnei Yisrael

On the tenth day of the month of Tishrei, on Yom Kippur, Hashem forgave all of Klal Yisrael for the sin of the *eigel*, and He said to Moshe, "סלחתי כדבריך—I have forgiven, according to your words!"[1]

Then Hashem handed over the second set of *luchos* to Moshe Rabbeinu, and Moshe came down from the mountain and announced the good news to the Yidden that Hashem had forgiven them.[2]

Moshe Rabbeinu had prayed to Hashem, "Ribbono Shel Olam, I beg you, make this day a day of forgiveness and atonement for the Jewish children every year," and Hashem agreed and appointed the day of Yom Kippur as the day He would forgive the Bnei Yisrael for their sins.[3]

That day, Hashem told Moshe that the Yidden should build a resting place for Him, a Mishkan where the Shechinah would rest among them.

The next morning Moshe gathered the Yidden and told them what Hashem had asked from them. He asked them to bring whatever they could that was necessary to build the Mishkan.[4]

During the forty days that Moshe Rabbeinu was on Har Sinai receiving the second set of *luchos*, the Yidden tried to fast every day. On the last day they increased their fast, planning to fast both day and night.

The next morning, they got up very early and wept very loudly opposite Moshe, and Moshe Rabbeinu wept back opposite them, until their combined tears went up to heaven and awakened mercy in Hashem. He said, "I swear that this crying will become a cry of joy, and this day will be turned into a day of forgiveness and atonement for all generations."[5]

As soon as Moshe came down from the mountain, the Yidden noticed that his face was shining with an extraordinarily divine light. Just as it is impossible for a person to look directly into the sun because of its great brightness, similarly the Yidden could not look directly at Moshe's face because of the great brightness. The Bnei Yisrael were very frightened.[6]

When Moshe Rabbeinu saw how frightened they were, he told them to come close to him. Aharon HaKohen and all the Nesi'im approached him. Moshe Rabbeinu gave them the good news that Hashem had reconciled with the Yidden and had given them the second set of *luchos*. When the rest of the Yidden saw and heard this, they also approached Moshe, and Moshe repeated his message to the whole nation.[7]

Moshe Rabbeinu did not know about the strong light that shone from his face, and when the Yidden informed him about it,[8] he took a cloth[9] and put it on his face as a mask to dim the great light, as not everyone could bear it.[10]

When Moshe Rabbeinu spoke with Hashem, he removed the mask from his face—likewise, when he learned with the Yidden, he would put the cloth back on his face.

When Moshe Rabbeinu came down from heaven with this divine shine on his face, the Bnei Yisrael felt very bad. "We are low because of our sin," they said, "and now Moshe's head is raised and ours is lowered!"[11]

On hearing this, Moshe went straight to Hashem and said, "Ribbono Shel Olam, when You made the Bnei Yisrael low, I lowered myself with them! Now that You have raised my head up again, please also raise up the heads of the Yidden!"

Hashem answered, "You are right! Go and raise up the heads of the Yidden!"

Moshe asked, "How shall I raise their heads?"

Hashem replied, "By counting them. This will show the love I have for them!"[12]

There is a parable about a king whose sheep were attacked by wolves. The king said to his shepherd, "Go and count the sheep, so that I know how many of them are missing!" This showed the shepherd how beloved the sheep were to the king.[13]

> The Ramban writes that when the Yidden were counted in the desert—besides the time when they had to give half a shekel to be counted—each Yid wrote his name on a piece of paper, and these were then given to Moshe. When Moshe looked at each name, that person was given a merit to live.

The Ramban writes that when the Yidden were counted in the desert—besides the time when they had to give half a shekel—each Yid wrote his name on a piece of paper, and these were then given to Moshe. When Moshe looked at each name, that person was given the merit to live.

The Ramban adds that when coming to the *tzaddik* Moshe and giving him his name in writing, the *tzaddik* would look at him with a good eye and would ask Hashem to show mercy on him.[14] It is said that this Ramban is the first source that relates to writing a *kvittel* with a name and giving it to a *tzaddik* in order to enable the *tzaddik* to *daven* for him.[15]

1 Rashi 33:11 2 Seder Olam Rabbah 6. 3 Tanchuma Pikudei 11. 4 Rashi beginning of Vayakhel. 5 Yalkut Shimoni Remes 391, Tanna d'Vei Eliyahu 2:4. 6 Pesikta Rabbasi 10. 7 Ramban 34:31. 8 Rashi Beitza 16:1. 9 Yonason 34:33. 10 Rashi 34 33. 11 Pesikta Rabbasi 10. 12 Bava Basra 10. 13 Rashi 30:16. 14 Ramban beginning of Parshas Bamidbar. 15 Bal Shemske, Ramban, Sefarim v'Sofrim Tzai.

Answer for Purim:
Question: Who was Hasach?
Answer: Daniel.

VAYAKHEL פרשת ויקהל

Question of the Week:
1. Where did the Nesi'im get the stones from?

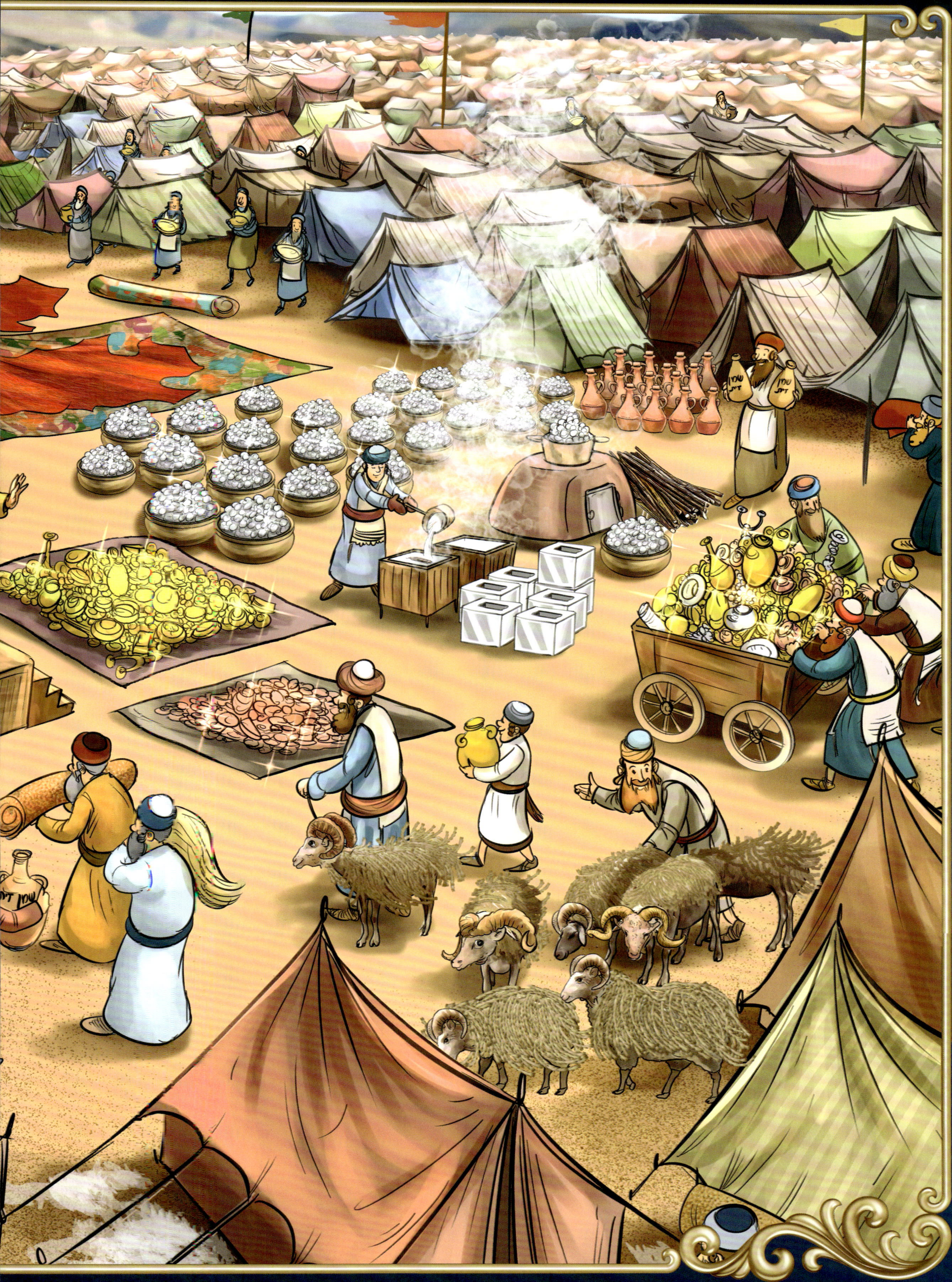

כל נדיב לב הביאו
Every good-hearted should bring

Hashem said to the Bnei Yisrael, "The reason I took you out of Mitzrayim was so you would build Me a tent, and I would have a place where My Shechinah would be able to rest among you."[1]

When Hashem told Moshe that He wanted the Yidden to build a Mishkan for Him, Moshe wondered, "The glory of Hashem fills the whole world! All the worlds below and above are filled with the glory of Hashem. And Hashem tells me to make a tent, a place for Him to live?"[2]

"Say to the Bnei Yisrael," Hashem answered, "it is not because I don't have a place to live that I ask them to build a tent for Me. My Beis HaMikdash was already built here above before I even created the world. It is only because of the love I possess towards my beloved children, the Jewish people, that I will leave my Beis HaMikdash from above and descend to rest among my beloved children below in Olam Hazeh!"[3]

When the Bnei Yisrael unfortunately sinned with the *eigel*, all the other nations rejoiced and began to tease the Yidden, saying, "The very nation that heard from G-d Himself 'אנכי—*I am Hashem…*' and 'לא יהיה לך—*It shall not be for you…*' only

A few hundred years earlier, in Mitzrayim, when Yaakov Avinu felt that the end of his life was approaching, he called his children together and said, "Dear children, you should know that a time will come when Hashem will tell you to build a Mishkan for Him. Be prepared for it!"

forty days later claimed that a calf was their god! Is there any hope for them?"

Moshe then begged and *davened* to Hashem that no *chillul Hashem* should arise through this, until Hashem said, "Go and tell the Yidden to build for Me a Mishkan, and through this I will raise their heads above all the nations of the world!"[4]

When Moshe told the Yidden to go and bring gifts because they were going to build a Mishkan for the Shechinah, they were filled with joy. There was running and rushing. Everyone raced with great enthusiasm to be the first to donate their possessions for the Mishkan. The force of the crowd was so strong that it was difficult to make order among the thousands of Jews who brought their donations.[5]

A few hundred years earlier, in Mitzrayim, when Yaakov Avinu felt that the end of his life was approaching, he called his children together and said, "Dear children, you should know that a time will come when Hashem will tell you to build a Mishkan for Him. Be prepared for it!"

The Yidden were indeed ready for this order, and as soon as Moshe arrived with the announcement to build the Mishkan, they already had their donations and immediately brought forward their prepared gifts so that they could begin to work on their long-awaited Mishkan immediately.[6]

Thirteen things were presented by the Yidden for the building of the Mishkan: gold, silver, copper, blue wool, purple wool, red wool, linen (flax), goat's hair, red dyed leather made from ram skin, leather made from seal skin, cedar wood, Shoham stones, and Milouim stones. All these things were needed either for the building of the Mishkan or for sewing the clothes of the Kohanim in the Mishkan.[7]

Besides these, the Yidden brought two more things: oil to be used to light the menorah, and spices that were needed for the incense and for the anointing oil.[8]

The Yiddishe women also participated in the *mitzvah* of donating to the Mishkan. They spun the wool with the hair, and this was used to sew the curtains in the Mishkan.

The learned women did a special thing. They did not cut off the hair from the goats (as was usually done) but spun the hair while it was still on the live goats.[9]

When Moshe announced to the Yidden the command to build the Mishkan, the Nesi'im said to Moshe, "We want to build the Mishkan only from our possessions!"

Moshe answered, "That is not what Hashem commanded. He wants every Yid to have a part in

> Thirteen things were presented by the Yidden for the building of the Mishkan: gold, silver, copper, blue wool, purple wool, red wool, linen (flax), goat's hair, red dyed leather made from ram skin, leather made from seal skin, cedar wood, Shoham stones, and Milouim stones. All these things were needed either for the building of the Mishkan or for sewing the clothes of the Kohanim in the Mishkan.

building the Mishkan, and every Yid should donate to it!"[10]

The Nesi'im decided, "Let the Yidden bring whatever they want to bring, and whatever is missing after that, we will bring."[11]

In barely two days, though, the Yidden had brought everything that was needed for the Mishkan.[12] So much so, that Moshe had a call sent out in the camp that they should stop bringing because there was already more than enough and no more was needed.[13]

As soon as the Nesi'im saw that no more material was needed, they were really upset. "Oh my. We are not partners at all in the Mishkan. What are we going to do now?" They donated the precious stones for the *choshen* and the *eifod*—the Shoham stones and the Milouim stones—which were still missing.[14]

1 Tanchuma Yashan Bechukosei 5. 2 Shemos Rabbah 34:1. 3 Tanchuma Yashan 51 19. 4 Pesikta Rabbasi, Pesikta d'Rabbi Kahane, Tanchuma. 5 Tanchuma Pikudei 11 6 Shemos Rabbah 33:8. 7 Rashi 25:2. 8 Sifsei Kohen 25:2. 9 Rashi 35 26. 10 Midrash HaGadol 35:27. 11 Sifrei Bamidbar Piska 45. 12 Tanchuma Yashan Teruma 3. 13 Shemos 36. 14 Avos d'Rabbi Nosson.

Answer to Parshas Ki Sisa:
Question: How many times were the Yidden counted in the desert?
Answer: Three times.

פרשת פקודי PIKUDEI

Question of the Week:
1. When was the Mishkan set up for the first time?

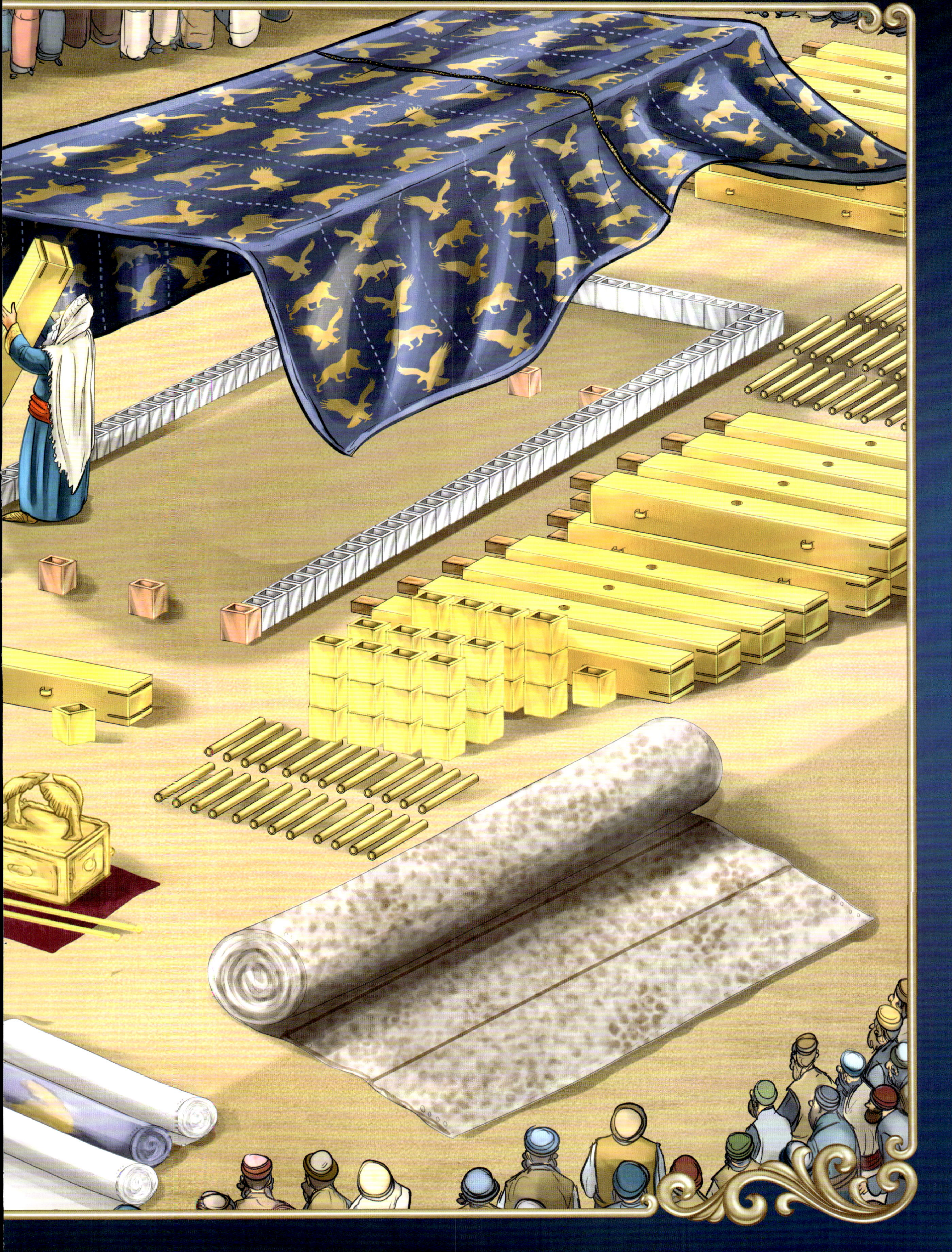

ויקם משה את המשכן
And Moshe lifted the Mishkan

On the twenty-fifth day of the month of Kislev (the first day of Chanukah), the Mishkan was completed. Although it was completed then, it was not set up until Rosh Chodesh Nissan, when it was erected by Moshe Rabbeinu.

The scoffers of the generation teased, "The Mishkan is ready. Why is it not being erected yet? It is probably flawed and is not exactly as Hashem wanted... and Hashem does not like it..."

However, they did not know what Hashem had in mind and what His solution was. Hashem did not want to mix the joy of erecting the Mishkan together with the joy that prevails in the month of Nissan because of the birth of Yitzchak Avinu.[1]

When the Mishkan was completed, the Yidden sat and waited. "When will the Mishkan be erected, and when will Hashem's Shechinah rest among us?"

When they saw that the Mishkan

Why were they not able to set up the Mishkan? Because Moshe Rabbeinu was very upset that he had had no part in building it. "The donations were brought by Klal Yisrael," Moshe complained, "the work was done by Betzalel and Ohaliav with the clever people... and what did I do?" Since Moshe Rabbeinu was saddened by this, Hashem hid from the Yidden, and they could not erect the Mishkan.

was not being set up, they were very sad. What did they do? They went to all those who had taken part in building the Mishkan and they said, "What are you waiting for? Set up the Mishkan and let the Shechinah rest among us!"

When the Chachamim tried to set up the Mishkan, they could not manage. Every time they tried, it fell down again. The Yidden went to Betzalel and Ohaliav and asked, "Come and set up the Mishkan, because Hashem has appointed you to build it."

Betzalel and Ohaliav took it upon themselves and began to erect the Mishkan, but they did not succeed either.

The Yidden began to complain: "What did Moshe do to us? We spent so much money on the Mishkan. We put so much *kochos* into it. What do we need it for? And Moshe said that Hashem wants to rest among us... So why don't we see this happening?"

Why were they not able to set up the Mishkan? Because Moshe Rabbeinu was very upset that he had had no part in building it. "The donations were brought by Klal Yisrael," Moshe complained, "the work was done by Betzalel and Ohaliav with the Chachamim... and what did I do?" Since Moshe Rabbeinu was saddened by this, Hashem hid from the Yidden, and they could not erect the Mishkan.

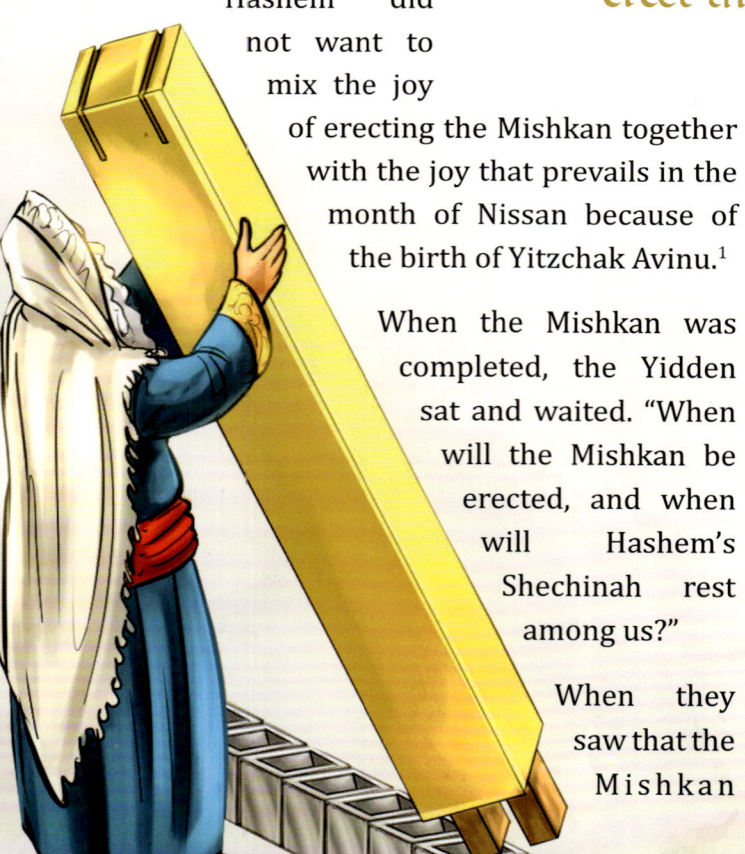

When the Yidden saw that what they were trying to do was not working, they went to Moshe and said, "We did everything you told us, and we brought everything you told us. Did we perhaps forget something? Or did we possibly do something we didn't need to? Everything is ready here." And they showed everything to Moshe and said, "Isn't this what you ordered us to do?"

Moshe answered, "Yes! This is indeed exactly as Hashem wanted!"

"If so, why is the Mishkan not yet standing?" the Yidden persisted. "Everyone has tried to set it up, even Bezalel and Ohaliav have tried, but nobody can manage."

Moshe was very disturbed by the words of the Yidden, until Hashem told him, "As you are upset for not taking part in the building of the Mishkan, no one is able to erect it. I wanted everyone to know that you Moshe will be the one to set it up!"

And so it was. When the time came to set up the Mishkan, it was Moshe who did so—alone, without any help from anyone.[2]

When Moshe Rabbeinu ordered Betzalel to build the Mishkan with the keilim, he first ordered him to make the keilim—the aron, the shulchan, the menorah, etc.—and only after that, the Mishkan itself, with the curtains, the boards, the sockets, etc.

1 Pesikta Rabbasi 6. 2 Tanchuma Pikudei 11. 3 Brachos 55. 4 Minchas 99, Sforno Shemos 40.

> Bezalel asked Moshe, "Is this the way one builds a house? The custom is the other way around: first you build the house, and then you make the *keilim*. Yet you are telling me to build the *keilim* first. Where are we going to put them?"

Bezalel asked Moshe, "Is this the way one builds a house? The custom is the other way around: first you build the house, and then you make the *keilim*. Yet you are telling me to build the *keilim* first. Where are we going to put them?"

Moshe said to Bezalel, "Were you in the shadow of Hashem when He spoke to me? This is what Hashem ordered. First the *keilim*, and then the Mishkan!"

That's why they called him Betzalel, because the word "Betzalel" means *bezal Kel* (in the shadow of Hashem).[3]

When the time came to set up the Mishkan, Moshe actually erected the Mishkan first, and only then placed the *keilim* inside. First he erected the lower curtains, the curtains of the Mishkan, and they miraculously hung in the air, then Moshe laid out the sockets (*adanim*) and placed the boards under the curtains.[4]

Answer to Parshas Vayakhel:
Question: Where did the Nesi'im get the stones from?
Answer: They came down from heaven in a cloud.

VAYIKRA פרשת ויקרא

Question of the Week:
1. Which of the four *avodos* does not have to be done by a Kohen?

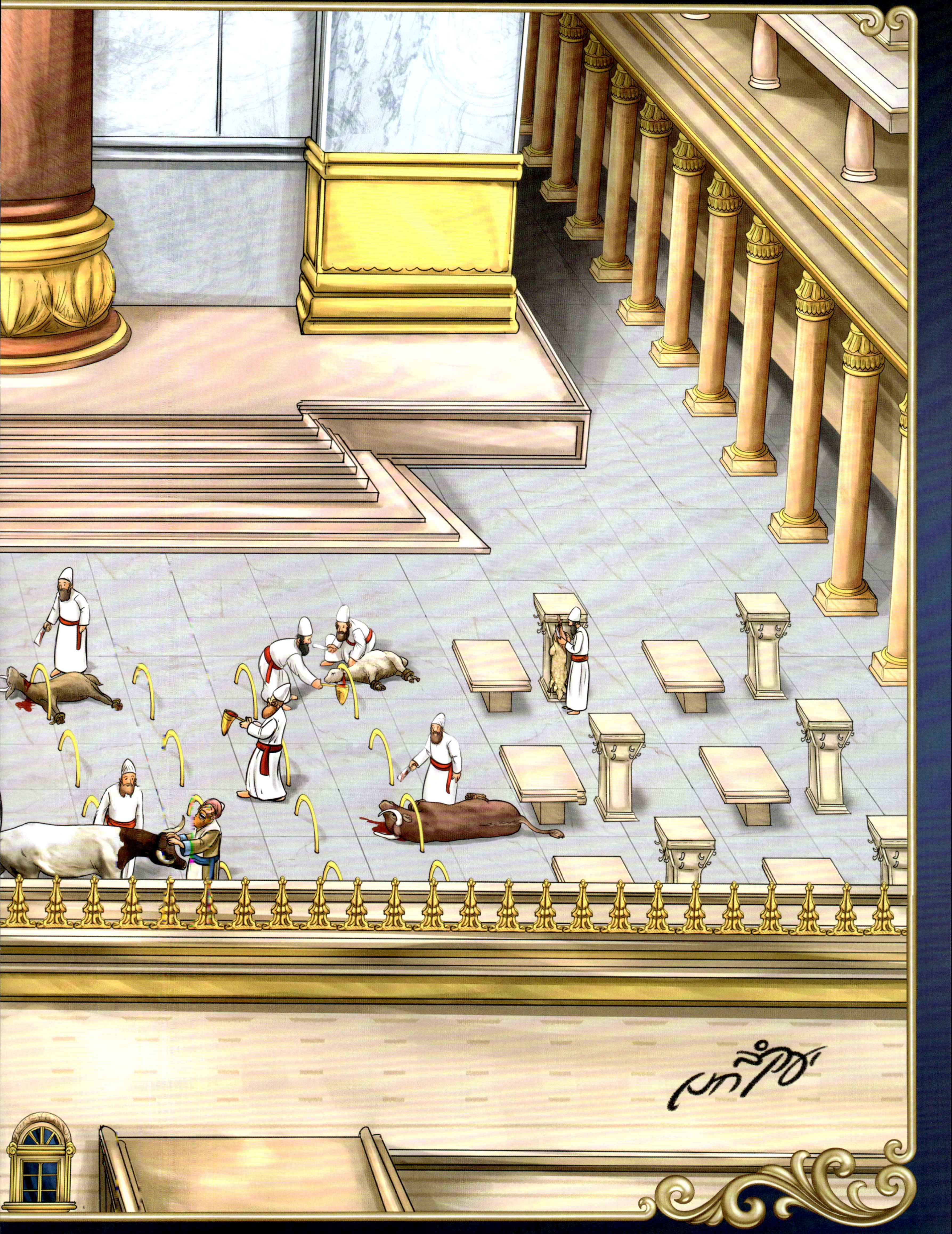

אם עולה קרבנו
If he brings an *olah* (burnt offering)

Now that there was a Mishkan, one could bring *korbanos* to Hashem. Indeed, Hashem taught Moshe the laws of all the various *korbanos* that would be offered in the Mishkan and in the Beis HaMikdash.

One of the *korbanos* was the *korban olah* (burnt offering). A burnt offering is usually not an obligatory sacrifice, which means that unlike a sin or guilt offering, which a person is obliged to make because of a sin he has committed, there is no sin for which a burnt offering is required as an atonement. A burnt offering is only offered as a donation. If one wants to sacrifice an offering of his own free will, then he donates an animal and dedicates it as a *korban olah*.[1]

(There are sacrifices of *olah* that one is obliged to bring, such as the *korban tamid*, *korban mussaf*, *korban olas re'iya*, and others, but these *korbanos* are not atonements for sins.)

One of the *korbanos* was a *korban olah* (burnt offering). A burnt offering is usually not an obligatory sacrifice, which means that unlike a sin or guilt offering, which a person is obliged to make because of a sin he has committed, there is no sin for which a burnt offering is required as an atonement. A burnt offering is only offered as a donation. If one wants to sacrifice an offering of his own free will, then he donates an animal and dedicates it as a *korban olah*.

In the *passuk*, however, it says that one must confess when one brings a burnt offering, and it is an atonement! Rashi says that there are certain sins for which the Torah does not obligate a *korban*, but when one brings *a korban olah* of his own free will, it can atone for the sin.[2]

A person who feels in his heart that he wants to bring a *korban olah* goes up to Yerushalayim, and he buys an animal there for a *korban*.[3]

An ox, a sheep, or a goat can be used as a *korban olah*. (One can also bring a bird *korban*, but our picture depicts an animal *korban*.)[4]

The day a Yid brings a *korban* in the Beis HaMikdash is a private Yom Tov for him, and he is forbidden to do any work on that day, just like during Chol HaMoed.[5]

Before he dedicates the animal as a *korban*, he examines it from head to toe to see if it has any blemishes, to make sure that the animal is kosher for a *korban*. Only then does he dedicate the animal for a *korban*, and it then receives a *kedushah* and is no longer allowed to be used for ordinary work (*meila*).[6]

In Yerushalayim there were experts who were well versed in examining an animal for a *korban*. The animals were brought to them to be checked, and they were paid a lot of money, as it was not an easy job.[7]

Immediately after entering the *azarah* (courtyard), the animal was given water to drink because it would be easier to skin it later.[8]

One then began to sacrifice the animal. There are many stages that are carried out with a *korban*, but four of them are important, and if not done correctly, the *korban* is invalid.

The four important stages that are executed in every *korban* are:

1. שחיטה—Slaughtering
2. קבלה—Collecting the blood into a vessel
3. הולכה—Transferring/carrying the blood to the *mizbeach*
4. זריקה—Sprinkling the blood onto the *mizbeach*

Let's look at these in order:

The first thing that needs to be done, before the slaughtering, is *semicha*.[9] This means that the owner of the *korban* leans himself on the head of the animal, between the two horns. He leans himself with all his might,[10] and at that moment he confesses,[11] repents for of all his sins, and asks forgiveness from Hashem, requesting that the *korban* be an atonement for him.[12] The *semicha* is conducted on the north side of the *azarah*, just before the slaughtering.[13]

Then the animal is slaughtered (שחיטה) on the north side of the *azarah* (the right side of the *mizbeach*),[14] and a Kohen stands ready with a vessel to receive the blood (קבלה).[15]

The Kohen then takes the blood in the vessel to the *mizbeach* (הולכה), and he sprinkles it on the two corners of the *mizbeach* (זריקה).

The order of sprinkling is as follows:

The Kohen stands on the floor and sprinkles the blood from the vessel onto the lower part of the *mizbeach*[16]—one sprinkle onto the corner from west to south, and the blood divides when sprinkling onto both sides of the *mizbeach*, the west and the south; and another sprinkle on the corner from east to north, in the same order.[17]

Then he pours out the excess blood onto the foundation of the *mizbeach*.[18]

After sprinkling the blood, the animal is hung up onto one of the poles located on the north side of the *mizbeach*[19] and the skin is peeled off,[20] preparing the animal to be sacrificed on the *mizbeach*.

Nothing is eaten from a *korban olah*; the whole animal is burned on the *mizbeach*.[21] The skin of the *korban* belongs to the Kohanim.[22]

---

1 Vayikra 1:2, Rashi. 2 Rashi 1:4. 3 Tosfos Menuchos 107. 4 Vayikra 1.5 Yerushalmi Pesachim 4:1. 6 Rambam Sefer HaMitzvos Lo Sa'asei 146.7 Bechoros 29. 8 Rambam Temidin u'Musafim 1:9. 9 Menuchas 92. 10 Chagiga 16, Menuchas 93. 11 Yuma 36. 12 Rambam Avodas Yom Hakipurim 82. 13 Menuchos 93, Zevachim 32. 14 Zevachim 5. 15 Zevachim 47. 16 Kinim 1. 17 Tamid 30, Yuma 15. 18 Zevachim 37. 19 Middos 3:5. 20 Zevachim 103. 21 Menuchos 74. 22 Zevachim 103.

Answer to Parshas Pikudei:
Question: When was the Mishkan set up for the first time?
Answer: 23 Adar.

פרשת צו TZAV

Question of the Week:
1. Which *korban* does Klal Yisrael bring together as a *korban todah*?

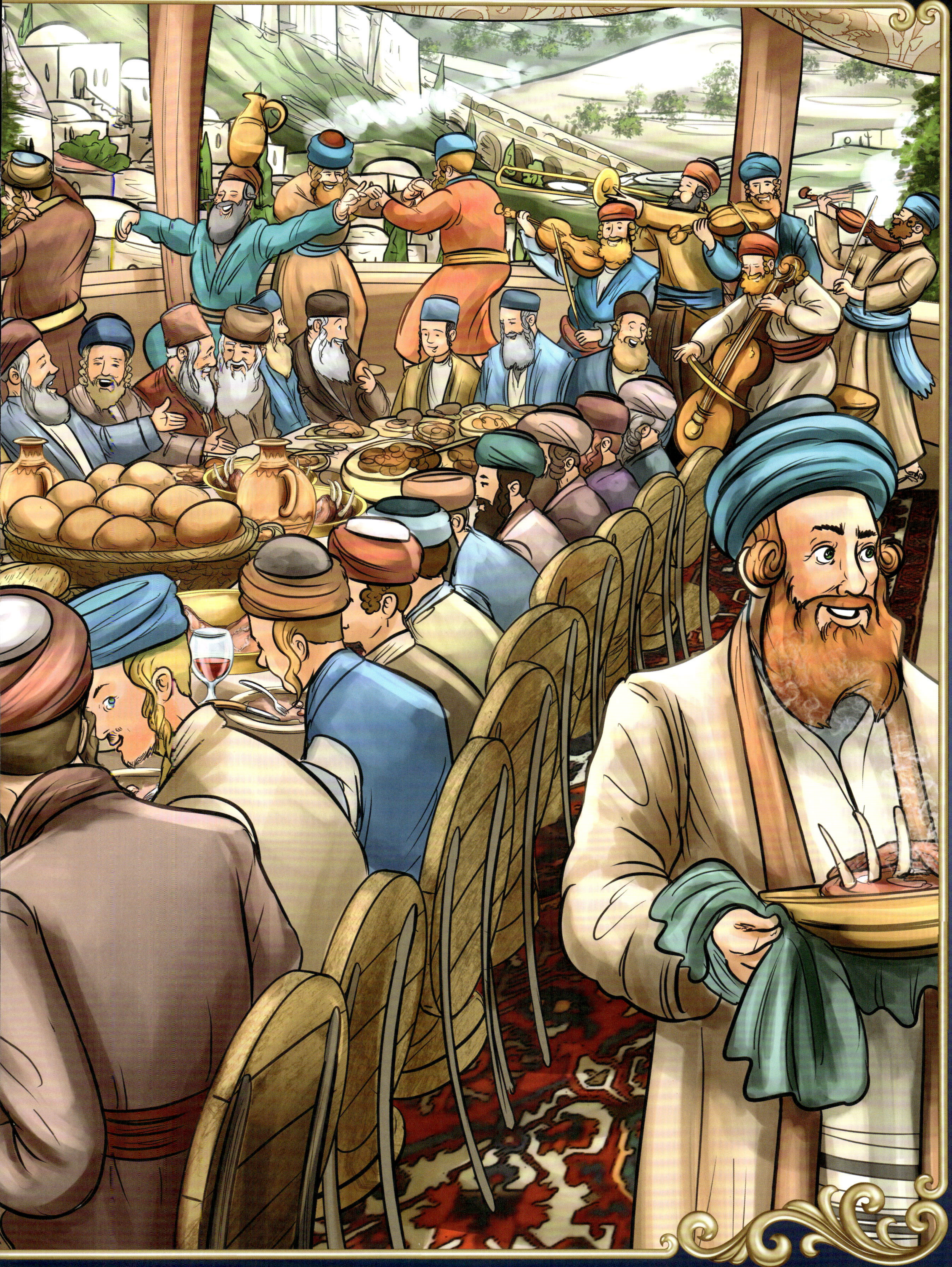

אם על תודה יקריבנו
If he offers it as a thanksgiving offering

"Ah, Zisha'le, it's good I met you," Reb Uriel calls out. "I'm just on my way to a *seudas mitzvah*. A good friend of mine invited me. If you want, you can come along."

"Are you sure?" Zisha'le asks in wonder. "You can just arrive at someone's *simchah* with uninvited guests?"

"Sure! What a question! Especially at this *simchah*. The more, the merrier! Come, let me explain more on the way.

"I'm sure you've heard of the *korban shelamim*, which is a *korban todah*,[1] yes?"

"Of course! It's a regular *korban shelamim* with a few exceptions," replies Zisha'le, as if he knows everything. "Firstly, you can only eat it on the day it has been offered, until midnight, unlike a *korban shelamim*, which may also be eaten the next day. Also, together with a *korban todah*—really *only* with a *korban todah*—one brings a *minchah*, the forty loaves of bread that are called *challos todah*."

"Right. Oh, we've already arrived," exclaims Reb Uriel. "Let's move nearer so that we can join in from close up."

"Wow, there is a lot of traffic. Just look at the musical instruments playing on all the corners of the street."[2] Zisha'le was excited. "A nice big crowd has gathered for the feast!"

"Right. You know, this is one of the reasons why the Torah allows eating a *korban todah* within such a short time. The purpose of bringing a *korban todah* is to thank Hashem for His kindness and miracles. The more people who join in, the more the glory of Hashem is exalted; and if the owner of the *korban* knows that in a few hours' time, whatever is left over from the *korban* may not be eaten, he will want to call as many people as possible to the feast, so that all the meat will be finished in time. This will cause the thanksgiving *korban* and *seudah* to be celebrated with much more ceremony, and the *kiddush Hashem* is very great."[3]

"Why is your friend bringing a thanksgiving *korban* today?" asks Zisha'le.

"Ah, one is obligated to offer a *korban todah* when he has been saved from danger.[4] Usually—as you surely know—danger refers to the four most dangerous events: sailing through the sea, traveling through the desert, illness, and being imprisoned.[5] But the truth is that it is not only when surviving these four things that one must bring a *korban todah*; any time a person is saved from danger he brings one[6]. After all, as a *korban todah* is essentially a *korban shelamim*—which means that one can donate it of their

"You see, Zisha'le, yesterday my friend Gavriel merited marrying off his youngest child, and that is why he is bringing a *korban todah* today. Look at him and you will notice that he is wearing his Shabbos clothes in honor of the *korban*. Look how happy he is, and how friendly and welcoming he is to all the guests who have come to join in his *simchah*."

own free will—it is normal that every time a person wants to thank Hashem for anything—whether he has a new baby, has made a good business deal, has made a good *shidduch*, or even if he just feels he wants to express praise and thanks to Hashem—he brings a *korban todah*.[7]

"You see, Zisha'le, yesterday my friend Gavriel merited marrying off his youngest child, and that is why he is bringing a *korban todah* today. Look at him and you will notice that he is wearing his Shabbos clothes in honor of the *korban*. Look how happy he is, and how friendly and welcoming he is to all the guests who have come to join in his *simchah*."

"I can see that the crowd is really happy for Reb Gavriel," Zisha'le says, very impressed. "Look how much meat has been prepared for the *seudah*… and look, just look… there on the table I can see the forty *lachmei todah*."

"Yes, and if you look closely, you will notice that the forty *challos* are divided into four types. That means there are ten *challos* of each type. Actually, thirty of them are *matzos*, without a single crumb of *chametz*, and the other ten are clearly *chametzdik challos*.

> *"Ahhh! Mazal Tov, Reb Gavriel!" Reb Uriel shakes his friend's hand warmly. "You should always be zoche to see only kindness from Hashem and to be able to bring many korban todos"*

"The *chametzdik challos* are easy to define, with their nice height, but the thirty other *matzos* are also divided into different types. Ten of them are called '*stam challos*,' or as others call it, '*matzos*', as there is no *chametz* in them. They are made with only flour, oil, and water and are baked in the oven, without being thinly rolled out. The other ten are called '*rekikin*.' These are kneaded with only flour and water, rolled out thinly, baked, and, only after the baking, spread with oil. Then we have the last group of ten *challos/matzos*, which are called '*revuchos*.' These are also kneaded with only flour and water, but they are only baked in the oven for a short while, after which they are fried in oil.[8]

"Something like the *panken* that we eat on Chanukah?" Zisha'le tries to understand.

"Similar, my child." Reb Uriel caresses his cheek lovingly. "I see that the crowd is enjoying the food. It seems to be very tasty. Let us join them before the *seudah* is finished."

"Ahhh! Mazal Tov, Reb Gavriel!" Reb Uriel shakes his friend's hand warmly. "You should always be *zoche* to see only kindness from Hashem and to be able to bring many *korbanos todos*!"

1 Mishna Menuchos 44. 2 Shavuos 15. 3 Netziv. 4 Zevachim 7. 5 Brachos 54. 6 Or Hachaim 219:9. 7 Midrash Tadshe 19. 8 Rambam HaKarbonos 89.

Answer from Parshas Vayikra:
Question: Which of the four *avodos* does not have to be done by a Kohen?
Answer: שחיטה

SHEMINI פרשת שמיני

Question of the Week:
1 What did Moshe wear while serving as a Kohen in the Mishkan?

הקהל

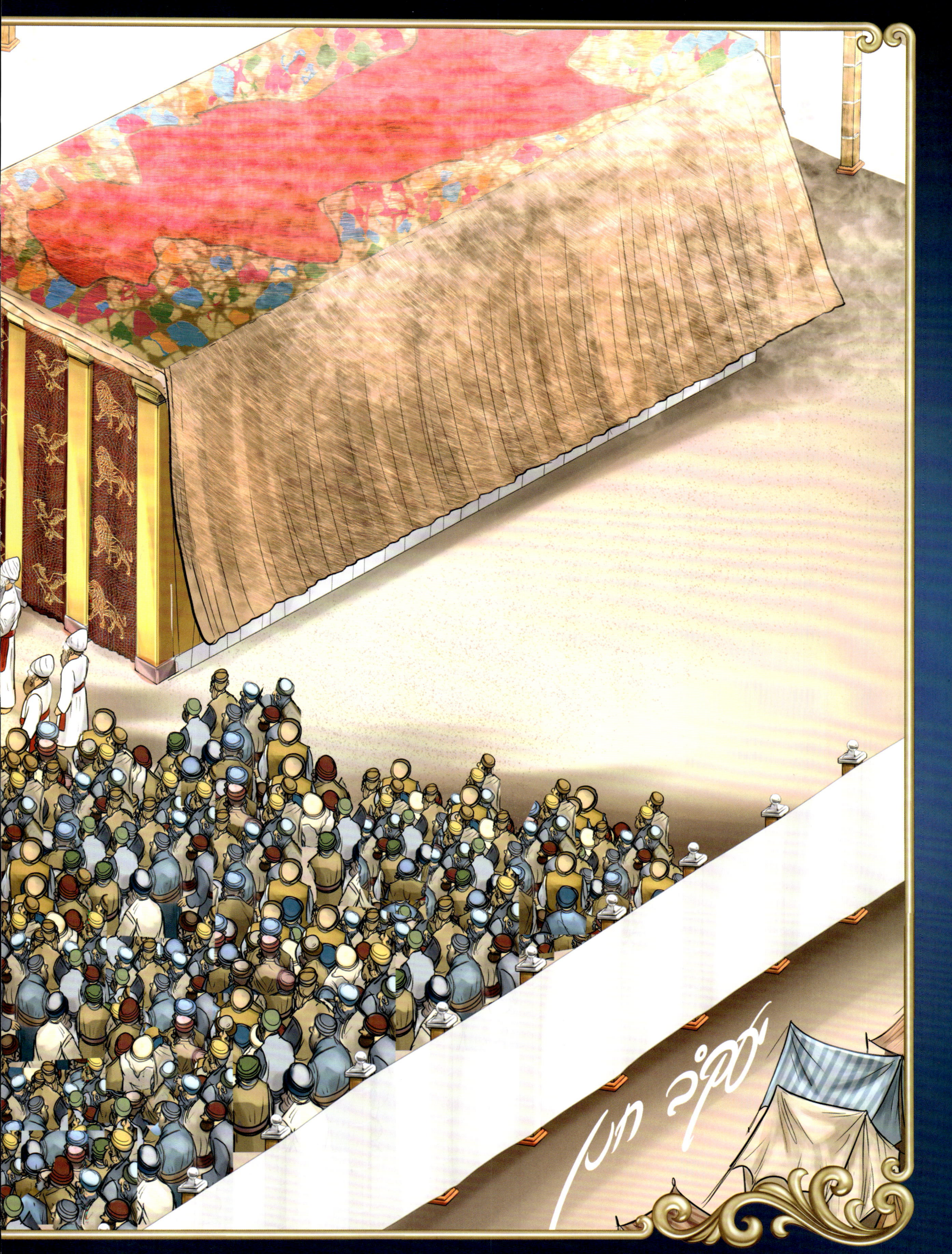

ויהי ביום השמיני
And it was on the eighth day

Each day, for seven days—the seven days of Milouim—Moshe Rabbeinu set up the Mishkan, acted as the Kohen Gadol and did the *avodah* inside,[1] after which he once again dismantled the Mishkan.[2]

During these seven days, Moshe Rabbeinu sanctified Aharon with his children so that they would become Kohanim. He anointed them with the oil of the Shemen HaMishchah, dressed them in the *bigdei Kehuna*, and let them watch how he did the *avodah* in the Mishkan.[3]

On the eighth day, Sunday, Rosh Chodesh Nissan,[4] Moshe Rabbeinu set up the Mishkan permanently, without dismantling it afterwards. That very same day, Hashem ordered Moshe Rabbeinu to sanctify Aharon HaKohen as the Kohen Gadol, and his four sons—Nadav, Avihu, Elazar and Itamar—as Kohanim, by bringing *korbanos*.

On that day, Rosh Chodesh Nissan, Aharon and his children did the *avodah* in the Mishkan, and Moshe Rabbeinu served as a normal Kohen together with them.[5] They all washed themselves and sanctified themselves with the water from the *kiyor*, and they did all the *avodos* together from that day. This was the day that the *Nesi'im* began to bring their *korbanos*.

On that day, Rosh Chodesh Nissan, Aharon and his children did the avodah in the Mishkan, and Moshe Rabbeinu served as a normal Kohen together with them. They all washed themselves and sanctified themselves with the water from the kiyor, and they did all the avodos together from that day. This was the day that the Nesi'im began to bring their korbanos.

the water from the *kiyor*, and they did all the *avodos* together from that day. This was the day that the *Nesi'im* began to bring their *korbanos*.[6]

Hashem told Aharon to bring a calf as a *korban chatas* (sin offering) and a ram as a *korban olah*. The calf was to be an atonement for the sin of the *eigel*[7] and the ram as a remembrance to the merit we have from Akeidas Yitzchak.[8]

Hashem did not tell only Aharon and his children to bring *korbanos*, but also the Bnei Yisrael. The Yidden were told to bring a goat as a *korban chatas*, a sheep and a calf as a *korban olah*, and an ox with a ram as a *korban shelamim*. The goat was to atone for the sin of selling Yosef (when the Shevatim dipped Yosef's shirt into the blood of a goat), the calf was to atone for the sin of the *eigel*, and the ram was a remembrance of Akeidas Yitzchak.[9]

"Moshe Rabbeinu," the Yidden asked very perturbed, "how can a nation serve their King when they never see Him? Did we go through so much trouble and effort for nothing? We thought Hashem would show Himself to us and dwell with us, and once and for all show us that He has forgiven us for the sin of the *eigel*."

"You are right," answered Moshe. "It is for this that you have put in so much effort. Today is the day you have been waiting for. Today, after you bring the *korbanos*, you will merit seeing the Shechinah resting among you!"[10]

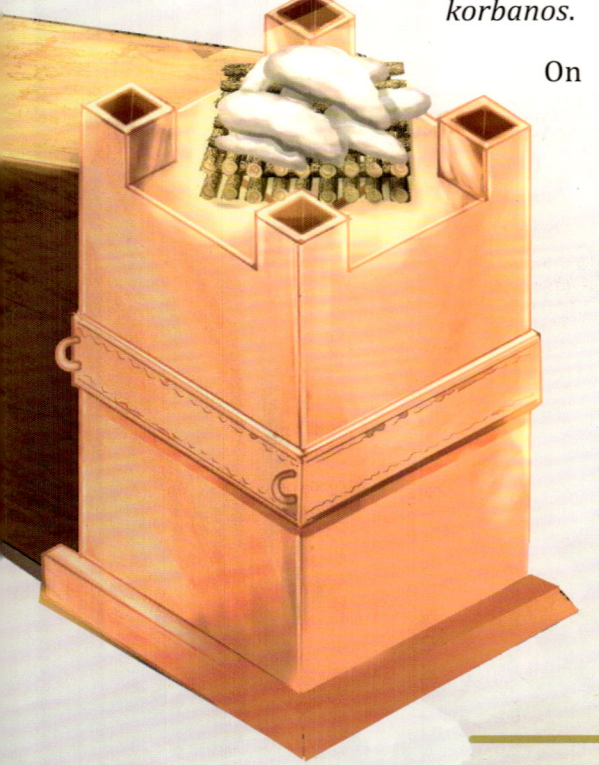

The Yidden acted with great alacrity and promptly did everything Hashem had ordered, and Aharon and his children slaughtered and laid the *korbanos* on the *mizbeach*.

As soon as Aharon saw that all the *korbanos* had been placed on the *mizbeach* and the Shechinah had not yet descended upon the Jews, he became very upset. "I know in my heart," he explained to himself with pain, "that because of me, the Shechinah does not come to rest among the Yidden. Hashem is angry at my sin, and therefore Klal Yisrael is does not merit the Shechinah."[11]

With great humility, he said to Moshe Rabbeinu, "This you did to me, my brother? That I should become so ashamed?"[12]

Moshe Rabbeinu went straight into the Ohel Moed, together with Aharon. They *davened* with all their might to Hashem and asked Him to have mercy on the Yidden.[13] They then went out to the courtyard of the Mishkan, where all the Yidden were gathered, and they blessed the people, saying, "May the will of Hashem be upon you, and may His Shechinah rest in everything you do!"[14]

Then the glory of Hashem appeared to the Yidden,[15] and wonderful miracles unfolded before their eyes. Hundreds of thousands of Yidden were gathered in the small courtyard around the Mishkan, when suddenly they saw the sky open and a fire come down like a pillar. It entered the Ohel Moed and went straight to the *mizbeach* and burned all the *korbanos* that were there. The fire then remained on the *mizbeach*.

When the Yidden saw all these wondrous events, they fell and bowed to the ground; miraculously, there was room for everyone. They saw clearly how the Shechinah had come to rest among them, and they sang and gave thanks to Hashem.[16]

1 Sifra 96, Mechilta DeMiluyim 1. 2 Seder Olam Rabbah 6. 3 Sifra, Rashi Vayikra 8. 4 Shabbos 87. 5 Rashi Shemos 40:31. 6 Seder Olam Rabbah 7. 7 Ramban Vayikra 9:2. 8 Yonasan 9:3. 9 Sifra Shemini 9:2. 10 Rashi 9:23. 11 Sifra 9:23. 12 Rashi 9:23. 13 Yonasan 9:23. 14 Rashi 9:23. 15 Yonasan 9:23. 16 Beraisa 49, Middos 4.

Answer from Parshas Tzav:
Question: Which *korban* does Klal Yisrael bring together as a *korban todah*?
Answer: The *korban Pesach* (Abarbanel).

פרשת תזריע TAZRIA

Question of the Week:
1. What is the difference between "בוהק" and "מספחת"?

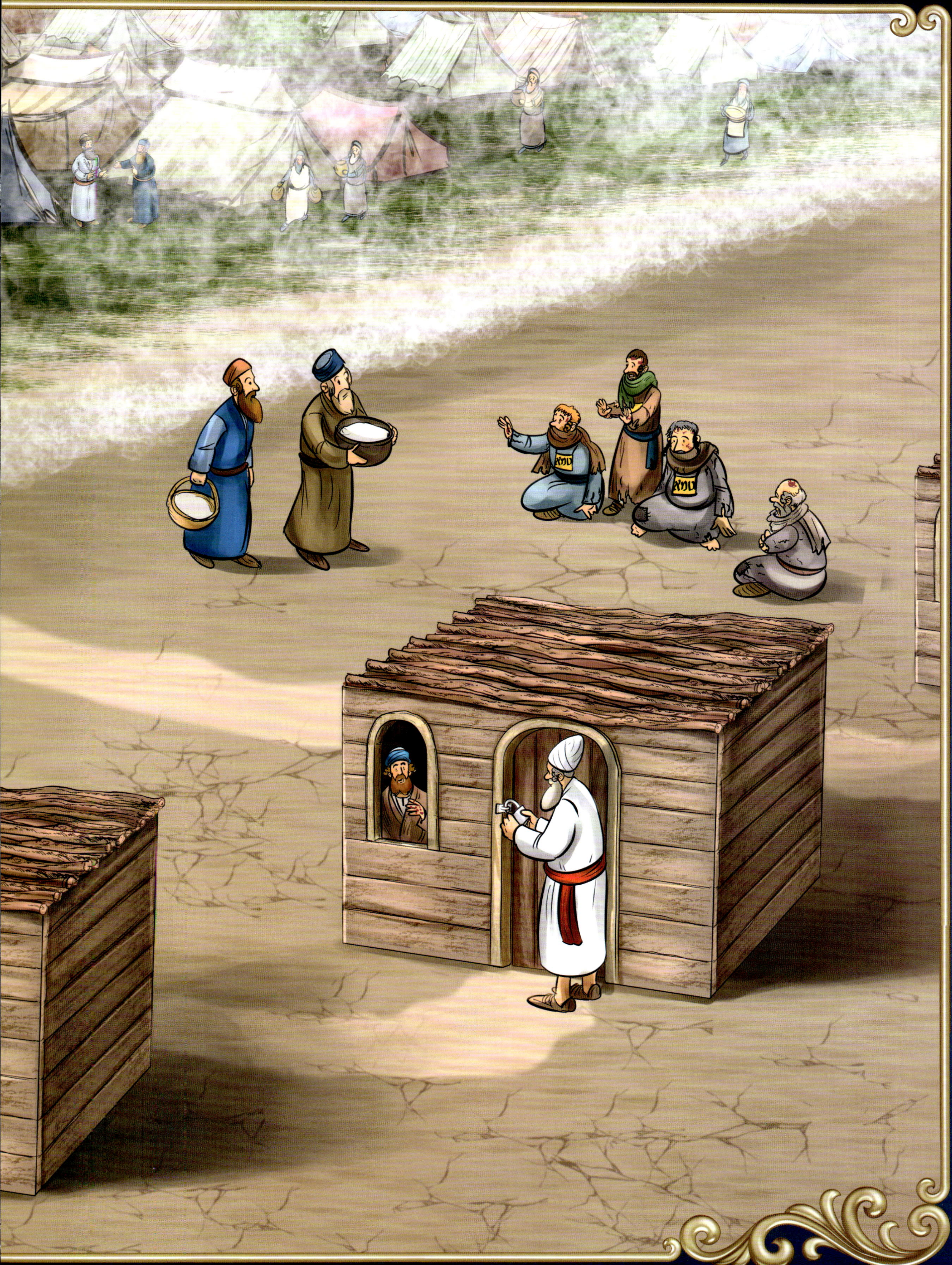

בדד ישב מחוץ למחנה
He shall dwell alone outside the camp

If a person saw a white spot on the skin of his body (not where the hair or the beard are) as big as a *gris* (six hairs by six hairs), he had to show it to the Kohen.

Only a Kohen could determine whether the person was *tamei* (impure) or *tahor* (pure). Even if the person was a *talmid chacham*, and he knew the *halachah* well, he still had to go to the Kohen.

Tzara'as is divided into two parts:

1. The way in which it is considered as *tzara'as* (the color and the size of the *tzara'as*).

2. The thing that comes to the *tzara'as*, through which it becomes a *tamei tzara'as* (the sign of *tumah*).

In order for it to be called *tzara'as*, the spot must have two conditions:

1. It has to have the color of *tzara'as*.

2. It must be the size of *tzara'as*.

If nothing has changed, he then has to remain in isolation for another seven days. As the first day of the second isolation period is also the last day of the first, he is in isolation for a total of thirteen days. After the second week has passed, he goes to the Kohen for the third time.

If the stain does not have one of the two conditions (color or size), then even if the stain has a sign of *tumah*, it will not be impure, because a sign of *tumah* is only impure if the stain has the conditions that make it *tzara'as*.

When the Kohen sees that both conditions of *tzara'as* (color and size) are present, he then looks to see if it also has a sign of *tumah*.

There are two signs of *tumah*:

1. White hair (two white hairs in the *tzara'as*).

2. A spot of raw flesh (healthy flesh—the appearance of normal skin—in the middle of the *tzara'as* (at least as big as two hairs)).

If he has *tzara'as* and in the middle he has one of the signs of *tumah*, the Kohen then declares him *tamei*. As long as the Kohen does not say clearly "You are *tamei*," he is not *tamei*—even if he has a definite *tamei tzara'as*.

If he has *tzara'as* but he does not have the signs of *tumah*, the Kohen isolates him for one week outside the camp. The Kohen does not check up on his *tzara'as* during these seven days.

When the seven days have passed, the *metzora* (the person with *tzara'as*) comes back to the Kohen a second time. Now there are three possibilities:

1. If the *tzara'as* has become darker, he is *tahor*, and if the *tzara'as* has become smaller than the minimum size of *tumah*, he is also *tahor*. However, since he has been in isolation, and anyone in isolation is *tamei*, he has to *toivel* himself and his clothes before he can become *tahor* and go home.

2. If the *tzara'as* has one of the three signs of *tumah*—white hair, a spot of raw flesh, or spreading—he is *tamei*.

3. If nothing has changed, he then has to remain in isolation for another seven days. As the first day of the second isolation period is also the last day of the first, he is in isolation for a total of thirteen days. After the second week has passed, he goes to the Kohen for the third time.

Now there are only two possibilities for the Kohen:

1. If there is now a sign of *tumah*—white hair, a spot of raw flesh, or spreading—he is still *tamei*.

2. If no change has occurred, and no signs of *tumah* have appeared, he may return home after he and his clothes have been *toiveled*, as he has been in isolation.

It is stated in *Toras Kohanim* that *tzara'as* is not just a regular spot, but a plague that hurts. It hurts so much that a sufferer cannot control his pain. He groans so much, that people know about it. (Certain Rishonim learn from here that if there is no pain, there is no *tzara'as*).

1 Radak, Onkelos.

The metzora who was declared tamei had different halachos than a metzora in isolation. The metzora who was declared tamei had to tear his clothes, remain bareheaded, was not allowed to cut his hair, and had to cover his mouth until his mustache. Besides needing to have some kind of sign on himself, he had to call out to anyone passing, "I am tamei," so that no one would come close to him.

The *metzora* who had to be in isolation outside the camp had to be completely alone, whereas the *metzora* whom the Kohen declared *tamei* was allowed to mix with other *tamei metzoros*, albeit outside the camp (according to Rashi).

When a *metzora* was told to go outside the camp, it meant outside Machene Yisrael. When they were living in Eretz Yisrael, it meant outside the walls that were put up in the time of Yehoshua ben Nun.

The *metzora* who was declared *tamei* had different *halachos* than a *metzora* in isolation. The *metzora* who was declared *tamei* had to tear his clothes, remain bareheaded,[1] was not allowed to cut his hair, and had to cover his mouth until his mustache. Besides needing to have some kind of sign on himself, he had to call out to anyone passing, "I am *tamei*," so that no one would come close to him.

Answer from Parshas Shemini:
Question: What did Moshe wear while serving as a Kohen in the Mishkan?
Answer: White clothes.

פרשת מצורע METZORA

Question of the Week:
1. Why are two birds taken for the *metzora*?

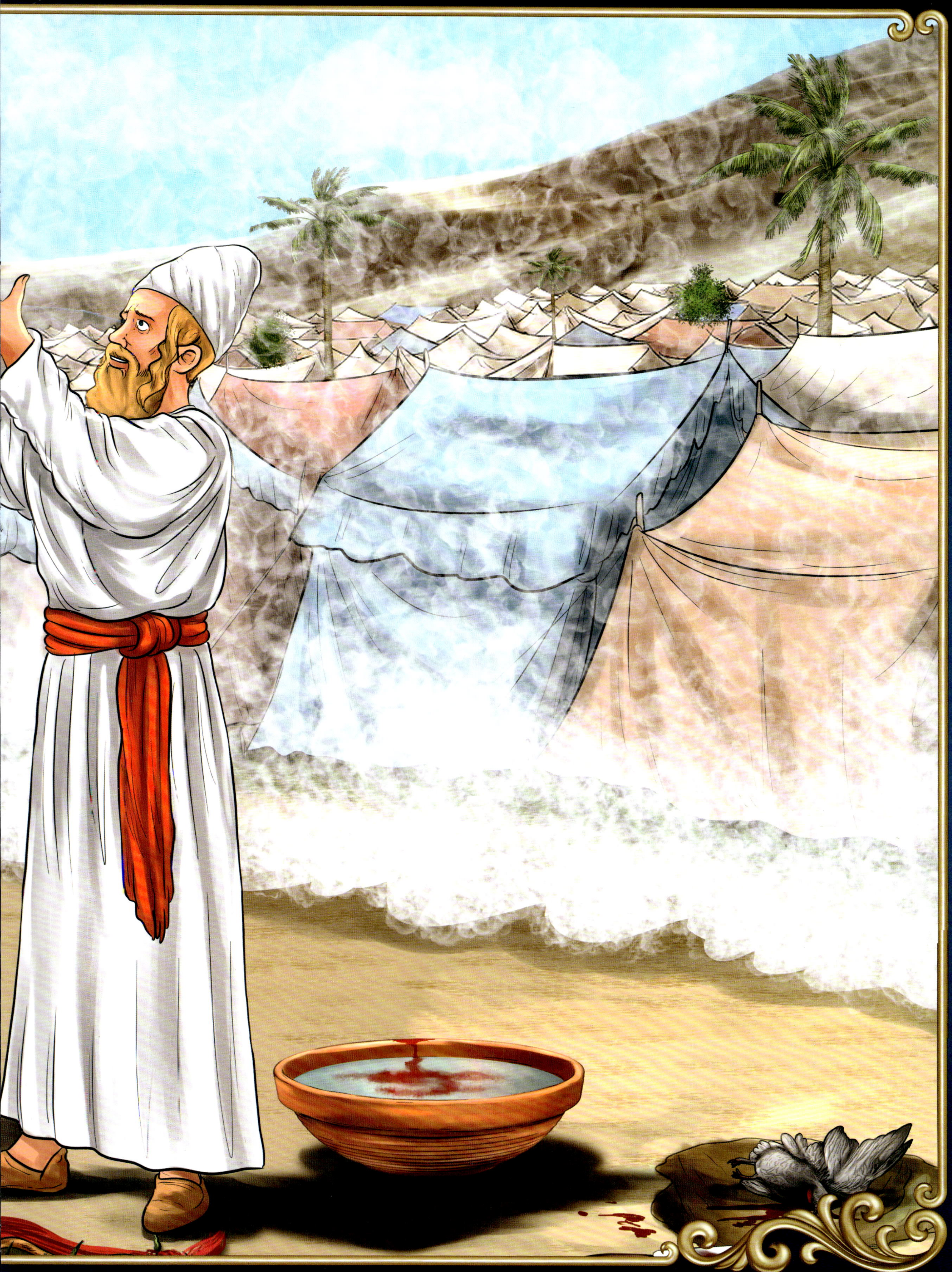

זאת תהיה תורת המצורע
This shall be the law of the metzora

Last week we learnt about a מצורע מוחלט (a *metzora* who was *tamei*), how he was sent outside all three camps, and how he had to dress.

In this week's *parshah* we learn what happens when the *tzara'as* disappears and the *metzora* is healed. The *metzora* lets the Kohen know that he has been cured.[1] The Kohen comes out from all three camps to the *metzora* and checks him to see if he is completely healed from *tzara'as*.[2]

When the Kohen sees that he is completely healed, the procedure of purification begins. The Kohen orders two kosher birds to be brought to him.[3] They both have to be the same size and the same value, and they must be bought together.[4] He also asks for a piece of cedar wood an *amah* long,[5] a hyssop twig,[6] and a string of red wool.[7] These do not need to be brought by the Kohen himself—they can be brought by anyone, even a Yisrael—but they must be brought in this order.[8]

The Kohen then chooses the better of the two birds[9] and orders a second Kohen[10] to slaughter the second bird.

The Kohen takes an earthen vessel and fills it with a quart of fresh spring water.[11] The water should not be dirty or salty, nor should it be warm or lukewarm; it should be fresh directly from its source.[12]

Then the Kohen slaughters the bird and lets the blood flow into the water in the earthen vessel. He then takes the three items mentioned above—the cedar stick with the hyssop twig and the red piece of wool—and he holds it together with the living bird[13] and dips it into the water mixed with the blood.

Using these three things, he sprinkles the water onto the *metzora* seven times on the outside of the hand, where you can see the nails.[14] Some say that he sprinkles the *metzora*'s forehead.[15]

While he sprinkles these three things, he ties the bird's wings to its legs, so that the it does not shake. This is to make sure that the *metzora* is not accidentally sprinkled through the bird rather than through the Kohen.[16]

The Kohen buries the slaughtered bird in the

ground in front of the *metzora*, as no pleasure can be had from it.¹⁷ (If the bird is left, it is feared that it might be eaten.) The Kohen sets the living bird free to fly away in the open field. When doing this, the Kohen does not face the city, nor does he face the sea; he lets the bird go free in the direction of the field outside the city.

It makes no difference in which direction the bird flies, but the Kohen must not be facing the city or the sea in order to send it there.¹⁸

There is a dispute regarding this. There are those who believe that the Kohen stands outside the city, and from there he sends the bird out to the open field,¹⁹ and there are those who say that while sending the bird out to the field, the Kohen had to stand inside the city and thus send it out of the city into the field.²⁰ How was this possible? The *metzora* was not yet *tahor*, so he could not yet enter the city. Tosfos answers that, according to this opinion, one derives that after spraying the *metzora*, the *metzora* actually remains outside the city, and only the Kohen enters, or the Kohen sends a messenger into the city to send the bird out of the city.²¹

According to this discussion, we see that everyone agrees that the metzora stays outside the city and may not enter, but there is a dispute about where the bird is set free. Either the Kohen stays outside the city, and from there he sends the bird, or he enters the city and sends it out to the field from there.

According to this discussion, we see that everyone agrees that the *metzora* stays outside the city and may not enter, but there is a dispute about where the bird is set free from. Either the Kohen stays outside the city, and from there he sends the bird, or he enters the city and sends it out to the field from there.

---

1 Chizkuni, R' Sadiah HaGoan, K'sav v'HaHabalah. 2 Vayikra 14:3. 3 Rashi 14:4. 4 Toras Kohanim, Leket, Rambam. 5 Nega'im 14:46. 6 Rashi Suko 13. 7 Rashi, R' Avraham Mizrachi in name of Rashi Bava Metziah 21. 8 Toras Kohanim, Or HaChaim HaKadosh. 9 Toras Kohanim, Rambam. 10 Toras Kohanim, Rambam, Malbim. 11 Rashi 14:5. 12 Toras Kohanim. 13 Bartenura Nega'im 14:1. 14 Rambam 11:1. 15 Discussion in Toras Kohanim. *Halachah* to sprinkle on palm of hand. 16 Minchah Balulo. 17 Nega'im 14:1, Rambam, Rashi, Bartenura. 18 Nega'im 14:2, Toras Kohanim. 19 Piskei HaTosfos 114. 20 Understood from Braiso, Rambam. 21 Tosfos Kiddushin 53.

Answer to Parshas Tazria:
Question: What is the difference between a "בוהק" and a "מספחת"?
Answer: A "בוהק" is definitely not *tzara'as*. Therefore, even if there are signs of *tumah*, he is not *tamei*. A "מספחת" is a normal *metzora*.

Answer to Parshas Metzora:
Question: Why are two birds taken for the *metzora*?
Answer: Birds chirp a lot, and *tzara'as* appears when a person speaks *lashon hara* (speaks too much).

Did you enjoy this book?
Looking forward to meeting you again in our next volume!

A VIEW ON THE PARSHAH

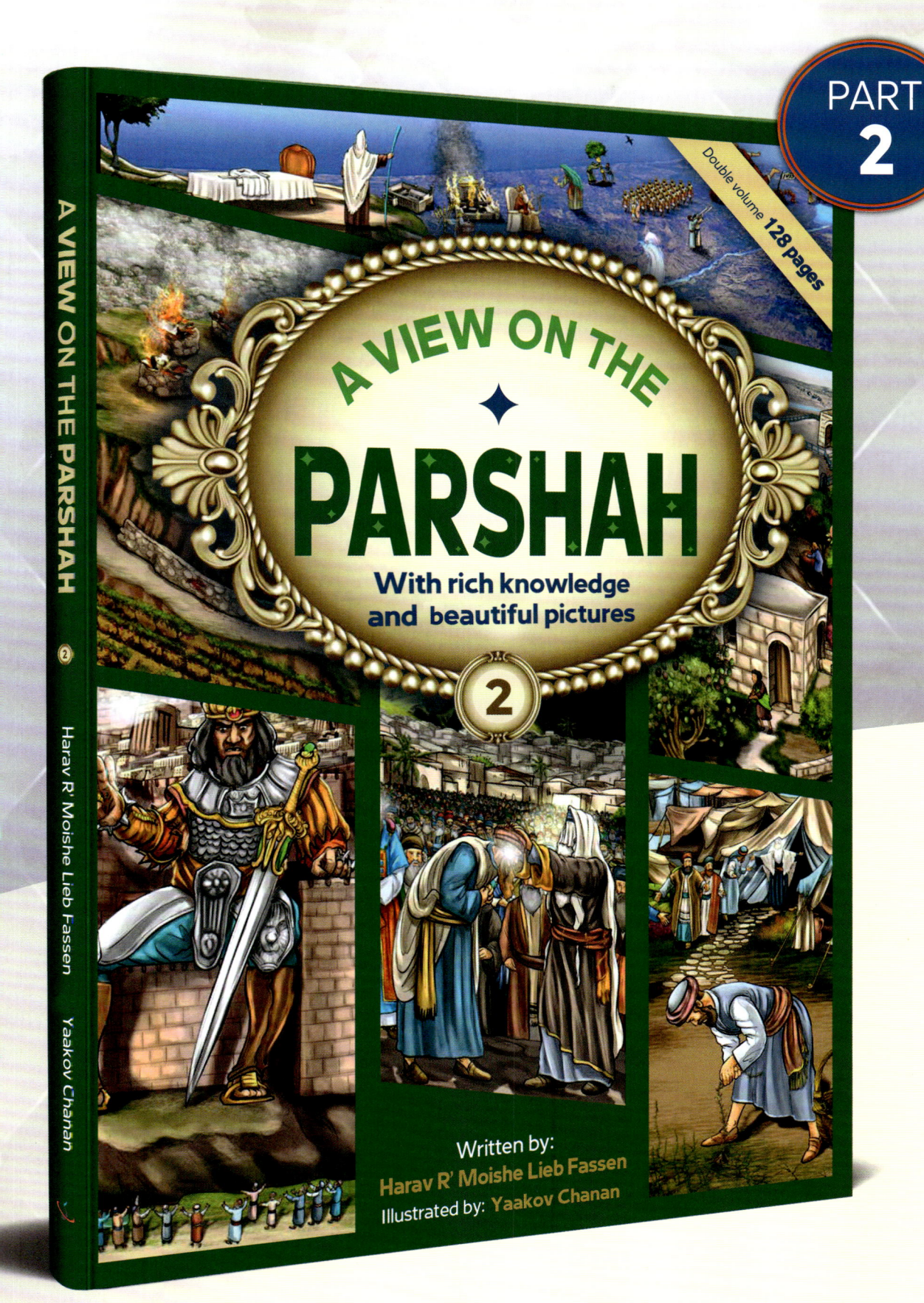

With rich knowledge and beautiful pictures

PART 2

Double volume 128 pages

Written by: Harav R' Moishe Lieb Fassen
Illustrated by: Yaakov Chanan